PUBLISHER COMMENTARY

The Department of Defense has embraced the concept of cloud computing in recent years and this approach has proven effective at reducing costs, That said, it is imperative that every possible security precaution be taken to ensure resiliency and survivability of the cloud and the data contained. The term "Cloud Service Provider (CSP)" can mean the on-site hosting CSP, off-premise hosting CSP, or a third party CSP offering cloud security services such as a Cloud Access Security Broker (CASB).

DoD's computer networks have always been targeted for cyber-attacks and now that includes the building controls systems (BCS). Defending a BCS is not as simple at protecting an IT network because most BCS consist of analog equipment that is decades old and retrofit to accept commands from modern digital controllers. Many BCS installations are a hodgepodge of technologies that should have been replaced years ago. DoD is well ahead of industry in this area because DoD recognizes it's a problem whereas most companies are blissfully unaware of their vulnerabilities.

We print a wide array of cybersecurity publications produced by the National Institute of Standards and Technology (NIST), Unified Facilities Criteria (UFC), Mil Handbooks and other publications that are directly applicable to the topic for consideration during the planning process. These publications cover a wide range of cybersecurity concepts that are carefully designed to work together to produce a holistic approach to cybersecurity primarily for government agencies and constitute the best practices used by industry. This holistic strategy to cybersecurity covers the gamut of security subjects from development of secure encryption standards for communication and storage of information while at rest to how best to recover from a cyber-attack.

Why buy a book you can download for free?

Some documents are only distributed in electronic media. Some online docs are missing some pages or the graphics are barely legible. When a new standard is released, an engineer prints it out, punches holes and puts it in a 3-ring binder. While this is not a big deal for a 5 or 10-page document, many cyber documents are over 100 pages and printing a large document is a time-consuming effort. So, an engineer that's paid $75 an hour is spending hours simply printing out the tools needed to do the job. That's time that could be better spent doing engineering. We publish these documents so engineers can focus on what they were hired to do – engineering.

Please visit our web site at https://usgovpub.com

Other books on cloud computing we print on Amazon.com

NIST SP 500-291	NIST Cloud Computing Standards Roadmap
NIST SP 500-292	NIST Cloud Computing Reference Architecture
NIST SP 500-293	US Government Cloud Computing Technology Roadmap
NIST SP 500-307	Cloud Computing Service Metrics Descriptions
NIST SP 500-325	Fog Computing Conceptual Model
NIST SP 800-144	Guidelines on Security and Privacy in Public Cloud Computing
NIST SP 800-146	Cloud Computing Synopsis and Recommendations
NIST SP 1800-4	Mobile Device Security: Cloud and Hybrid Builds
NIST SP 1800-19	Trusted Cloud
NISTIR 7904	Trusted Geolocation in the Cloud: Proof of Concept Implementation
NISTIR 8006	NIST Cloud Computing Forensic Science Challenges
NIST Whitepaper Adoption	Challenging Security Requirements for US Government Cloud Computing
White House	Federal Cloud Computing Strategy
DISA	Cloud Computing Security Requirements

A Combat Support Agency

DEPARTMENT OF DEFENSE (DoD)

CLOUD CONNECTION PROCESS GUIDE

Version 2
March 2017
Defense Information Systems Agency
Risk Executive (RE)
Risk Adjudication and Connection Division

Post Office Box 549
Fort Meade, Maryland 20755-0549
http://disa.mil/connect

This page intentionally left blank

EXECUTIVE SUMMARY

The Cloud Connection Process Guide (Cloud CPG) expands the Defense Information Systems Network Connection Process Guide (DISN CPG) to include guidance for Department of Defense (DoD) connection and use of Cloud computing services. The goal of the Cloud CPG is to help a Cloud Service Provider (CSP) navigate the DoD's process for connecting a Cloud Service Provider-Cloud Service Offering (CSP-CSO) to the DISN and make it available for use by DoD Mission Owners. The Cloud CPG also helps a DoD Component[1] Mission Owner to connect to an authorized CSP-CSO and "on-board" (or implement) a DoD Cloud Information Technology Project (C-ITP) in accordance with DoD cloud policy.

Section 1 of this guide provides an introduction and overview of the DoD Cloud Computing Environment and associated terms used within the DoD Cloud Community. Section 2 provides guidance to CSPs and their DoD Sponsors for registering and connecting Information Impact Levels 2, 4, and 5 CSP-CSOs to the DISN. Section 3 provides guidance to DoD Mission Owners for registering and opening a connection to an authorized CSP-CSO. Appendix H provides guidance for Classified (Information Impact Level 6) cloud connections.

Nothing in this Cloud CPG is intended or designed to usurp or impede: a DoD Component's authorities to develop and implement its own compliant cloud strategies under Title 10; or an Authorizing Official's (AO) authorities under DoD Instruction (DoDI) 8500.01 (ref a) and DoDI 8510.01 (ref b). In addition, nothing in this Cloud CPG alters or supersedes the existing authorities and policies of the Director of National Intelligence (DNI) regarding the protection of sensitive compartmented information (SCI), as directed by Executive Order 12333 and other laws and regulations.

This release of the Cloud CPG reflects the evolution of the DoD cloud strategy. This document incorporates the lessons learned and process insights from "cloud pilots" and various other efforts. DISA will update this guide to comply with DoD CIO Memo, *Updated Guidance on the Acquisition and Use of Commercial Cloud Computing Services* (ref c), and the DoD Cloud Computing Security Requirements Guide (Cloud SRG) (ref d).[2]

Please send your improvement comments directly to the DISA Connection Approval Office (CAO) at disa.meade.ns.mbx.ucao@mail.mil or disa.meade.ns.mbx.ccao@mail.mil and the DISA Cloud Services Support Office (DISA CSSO) at disa.meade.re.mbx.disa-commercial-cloud@mail.mil.

The instructions in this guide are effective immediately and publically available from the DISA website at http://disa.mil/computing/cloud-services.

---

[1] The term "Components" collectively refers to OSD; the Military Departments; the Office of the Chairman of the Joint Chiefs of Staff (CJCS) and the Joint Staff; the Combatant Commands; the Office of the Inspector General of the DoD; the Defense Agencies, the DoD Field Activities; and all other organizational entities within the DoD.

[2] The DoD Cloud Computing Security Requirements Guide (Cloud SRG (ref d)) and related documents are at: http://iase.disa.mil/cloud_security/Pages/index.aspx

---

SIGNATURE PAGE

Approved by:

_____   _____

Matthew A. Hein   Date

Chief, Risk Adjudication and Connection Division

REVISION HISTORY

DISA will review and update this document as needed. The revision history table documents significant changes to this guide.

Version	Date	Revisions
1.0	21 Aug 2015	• Initial Release • The emphasis was registration of CSPs and DoD C- ITPs in the DISA SNAP Database <u>(ref e)</u>
1.01	22 Sep 2015	• Incorporated guidance from the DISA Document Release Group (DRG) to authorize public release
2.0	March 2017	• Approved draft for formal review and comment • Expands the scope from a DISA to a DoD Cloud Process Guide • Reorganizes the material by major cloud processes: CSP-CSO Registration and Connection, Sustaining, Services Discontinuation; and, C-ITP Registration and Connection, Sustainment, and Service Discontinuation • Presents processes in a step-by-step fashion • Adds appendices for DoD Component Cloud Connection, Cloud Points of Contact, Classified C-ITP Registration, and documentation requirements

Please send comments on the DoD Cloud CPG to the DISA CSSO at <u>disa.meade.re.mbx.disa-commercial-cloud@mail.mil</u>

TABLE OF CONTENTS

LIST OF FIGURES

LIST OF TABLES

This page intentionally left blank

SECTION 1: INTRODUCTION

1.1 Purpose

The Cloud CPG provides guidance, points of contact, and processes for a Cloud Service Provider (CSP) to connect a Cloud Service Provider-Cloud Service Offering (CSP-CSO) to the DISN and to make the CSP-CSO available for use by DoD Mission Owners. The guide also provides guidance for a Mission Owner to register and open a connection to an authorized CSP-CSO and "on-board" (or implement) a Cloud Information Technology Project (C-ITP) within an authorized CSP-CSO.

1.2 Authority

The Cloud Connection Process Guide (CPG) derives its authority from the same sources as the *DISN Connection Process Guide* (DISN CPG) (ref f) . Further, the DoD CIO Memo, *Updated Guidance on the Acquisition and Use of Commercial Cloud Computing Services* (ref c) establishes authorities and guidance for Commercial Cloud Computing Services. Finally, the DoD Cloud SRG (ref d) outlines the security controls and requirements necessary for using cloud-based solutions within the DoD and states that the DoD Cloud CPG defines responsibilities needed to establish and maintain connections between CSP-CSOs and DoD C-ITPs.

1.3 General Guidance

The Cloud CPG is a living document that will continue to evolve as connection processes are refined and as additional cloud computing services become available. This version of the Cloud CPG focuses on processes for connecting CSP-CSOs and DoD C-ITPs via the DISN. DISA will integrate the Cloud CPG into future versions of the DISN CPG (ref f). Additional information about DISA enterprise cloud computing services is at http://www.disa.mil/Computing/Cloud-Services.

Use the DoD Cloud CPG to help get through the connection process. However, before employing this guide, always check for the current version at website: http://disa.mil/connect.

1.4 Applicability

This guide applies to all Mission Owners and Cloud Service Providers involved in using or offering cloud computing services.

1.5 Background

In the current political, economic, and technological landscape, information technology (IT) will continue to provide extensive and ever-increasing capabilities while consuming fewer resources. With the increase of both state-sponsored and independent cyber threats, the DoD recognizes the growing importance of leading a strong and secure presence in cyberspace while responding to the need for continued budgetary constraints and stricter financial oversight. As a result, the Department must transform the way in which it acquires, operates, and manages its IT in order to realize increased efficiency, effectiveness, and security (ref g).

The Department has begun this transformation by establishing a set of initiatives aimed at achieving improved mission effectiveness and cybersecurity in a reengineered information infrastructure. The result of this new effort will be the Joint Information Environment (JIE), which delivers faster, better-informed collaboration and decisions enabled by secure, seamless access to information regardless of computing device or location.

The DoD cloud computing environment is a key component to enable the Department to achieve JIE end state of an agile, secure, and cost effective service environment that can rapidly respond to changing mission needs. Cloud computing will enable the Department to: consolidate and share commodity IT functions resulting in a more efficient use of resources; enhance Warfighter mobility through device and location independence; provide on-demand secure global access to mission data and enterprise services; and provide increased opportunity for rapid application development and reuse of applications acquired by other organizations.

The Department has specific cloud computing challenges that require careful adoption considerations, especially in areas of cybersecurity, continuity of operations, information assurance (IA), and resilience. To help meet these challenges, the Department is leveraging the Federal Risk and Authorization Management Program (FedRAMP) (ref h) which serves as the minimum security baseline for DoD and provides a standardized approach to security assessment, authorization, and continuous monitoring focused on enabling secure cloud computing products and services. DoD Components may host DoD Unclassified DoD information that is publically releasable on FedRAMP approved cloud computing services that have a DoD Provisional Authorization (PA) as described in this document and the DoD Cloud SRG (ref d).

For more sensitive DoD unclassified data or IT Projects, DoD established the FedRAMP+ concept for leveraging the work done as part of FedRAMP assessment by adding specific security controls and requirements necessary to meet and assure DoD's critical mission requirements as specified in the DoD Cloud SRG (ref d).

1.6 Key Concepts and Terminology[3]

This document uses the following terms defined in DoD, CNSS, and NIST publications [4] related to DoD cloud computing.

Assessor (aka Auditor) a party accredited to conduct independent assessment of cloud computing services, information system operations, performance, and security of the cloud implementation.

Boundary Cloud Access Point (BCAP) establishes a protected boundary between the DISN and a CSP-CSO. A BCAP will provide the capability to detect and prevent a cyber-attack from reaching the DODIN. The BCAP Functional Requirements Document (FRD) (ref i) describes the architecture of a DoD-approved BCAP. The DoD CIO must approve a DoD Component BCAP in accordance with procedures in Appendix C.

Carrier – provides connectivity and transport of cloud computing services from providers to Mission Owners (e.g., DISN).

---

[3] See NIST Special Publication, NIST SP 800-145 online at http://dx.doi.org/10.6028/NIST.SP.800-145

[4] NIST Cloud Computing Related Documentation online at http://www.nist.gov/itl/cloud/publications.cfm

---

Cloud Service Offering (CSO): a Cloud Service Provider's product or service. A CSO may be a combination of multiple product/service offerings (e.g., Microsoft O-365 and Azure) and it can be based on any of the Cloud Deployment Models or Cloud Service Models (see below).

Cloud Service Provider (aka Cloud Provider): an organization that provides cloud computing services – a CSP can be a business, a DoD Component, or another Federal Department or Agency.

Cloud IT Project (C-ITP): a Mission Owner's project that implements a machine, software application, or information service within one or more authorized CSP-CSOs and is registered in DISA SNAP (ref e) using the same project name the Mission Owner gave the C-ITP in the SNaP-IT and DITPR databases.

Connectivity/Transport – The DISN (NIPRNet, SIPRNet)

Deployment Models[5]: A cloud computing system may be deployed privately or hosted on the premises of a cloud customer, may be shared among a limited number of trusted partners, may be hosted by a third party, or may be a publically accessible service, that is., a public cloud. The different deployment models present a number of tradeoffs in how customers can control their resources, and the scale, cost, and availability of resources (ref j).

- *Private cloud.* The cloud infrastructure is provisioned for exclusive use by a single organization comprising multiple Mission Owners (e.g., business units). It may be owned, managed, and operated by the organization, a third party, or some combination of them, and it may exist On-Premise or Off-Premise.

- *Community Cloud.* The cloud infrastructure is provisioned for exclusive use by a specific community of Mission Owners from organizations that have shared concerns (e.g., mission, security requirements, policy, and compliance considerations). It may be owned, managed, and operated by one or more of the organizations in the community, a third party, or some combination of them, and it may exist on or Off-Premises.

- *Public cloud.* The cloud infrastructure is provisioned for open use by the general public. It may be owned, managed, and operated by a business, academic, or government organization, or some combination of them. It exists on the premises of the cloud provider.

- *Hybrid cloud.* The cloud infrastructure is a composition of two or more distinct cloud infrastructures (private, community, or public) that remain unique entities, but are bound together by standardized or proprietary technology that enables data and application portability (e.g., cloud bursting for load balancing between clouds)."

---

[5] See NIST Special Publication, 800-146 for a Cloud Computing synopsis, recommendations, and terminology online at http://nvlpubs.nist.gov/nistpubs/Legacy/SP/nistspecialpublication800-146.pdf

DoD Assessor A DoD organization that leverages any existing Joint Assessment Board (JAB), Federal Agency, or DoD Self-Assessed PA and assesses CSP-CSOs for compliance with FedRAMP+ requirements as stipulated in the DoD Cloud SRG (ref d) (e.g., DISA Cloud Assessment Team, DoD Component Cloud Assessor).

DoD Sponsor: DoD Component responsible for ensuring the connection or CSP-CSO has a valid DoD mission essential requirement, is properly maintained, resourced and secure throughout the cloud connection's lifecycle. The DoD Sponsor and DoD Mission Owner can be one in the same. The responsibilities of DoD sponsors are defined in several OSD and Joint Staff issuances and are summarized in the DoD CIO *Summary of DoD Sponsor Responsibilities for Mission Partner Connections to the Defense Information Systems Network (DISN),* Memorandum, 14 August 2012

Information Impact Levels: Information Impact Levels are defined by potential impact of an event resulting in the loss of confidentiality, integrity, or availability of data, systems or networks. See Section 3 of the DoD Cloud SRG (ref d) for details:

- **Information Impact Level 2 -** includes all data cleared for public release, as well as some DoD private unclassified information not designated as Controlled Unclassified Information (CUI) or critical mission data, but the information requires some minimal level of access control.

- **Information Impact Level 4 -** accommodates CUI or other mission critical data that a law, regulation, or Government-wide policy requires, or specifically permits, an agency to handle by means of safeguarding or dissemination controls.

- **Information Impact Level 5 -** accommodates CUI that requires a higher level of protection than that afforded by Level 4 as deemed necessary by the information owner, public law, or other government regulations. Level 5 also supports unclassified National Security Systems (NSSs).

- **Information Impact Level 6 -** accommodates information that has been determined: (i) pursuant to Executive Order 13526, *Classified National Security Information* (December 29, 2009), or any predecessor Order, to be classified national security information; or (ii) pursuant to the Atomic Energy Act of 1954, as amended, (P.L. 83-703) to be Restricted Data (RD).

Internet Access Point. An IAP establishes a protected boundary between the NIPRNet and the public Internet. An IAP has capabilities to detect and prevent a cyber-attack on the NIPRNet from the Internet.

Mission Owner (aka Cloud Consumer): - Person or organization that maintains a business relationship and uses (or intends to use) authorized CSP-CSOs.

On-Premise and Off-Premise CSP-CSO - Figure 1 illustrates how CSP-CSOs connect to the DISN when operating within a non-DoD facility (Off-Premise) or when operating within a DoD facility (On-Premise[6]) . On-Premise CSP-CSOs connect to the DISN via

---

[6] DoD Cloud SRG (ref d): CSP Infrastructure (dedicated to DoD) located inside the Base/Post/Camp/Station (B/C/P/S) "fence-line" (i.e., On-Premise) connects via an Internal CAP (ICAP). The architecture of ICAPs may vary and may leverage existing capabilities such as the cybersecurity stack protecting a DoD Data center today or may be a Joint Regional Security

Internal CAPs (ICAPs). Off-Premise CSP-CSOs used for publically releasable data (Information Impact Level 2) usually connect to the Internet and interoperate with users on the NIPRNet via a NIPRNet Internet Access Point (IAP). Off-Premise CSP-CSOs used for Sensitive Data (Information Impact Levels 4 or 5) connect to the NIPRNet through a DoD CIO-approved BCAP such as the DISA Enterprise BCAP or a DoD Component BCAP (e.g., the Navy BCAP) in accordance with the *DoD Cloud SRG* (ref d). Each CAP must implement boundary protections as defined in the *DoD Cloud SRG* (ref d) and the *DoD Secure Cloud Computing Architecture (SCCA) Functional Requirements (FR)* (ref k) to detect and prevent a cyber-attack from reaching the DODIN. As illustrated in Figure 1:

- All CSP-CSOs and Mission Owner C-ITPS must be registered in the DISA SNAP system (ref e) in accordance with DoD policy (ref c) and this guide.

- Information Impact Level 4 and 5 CSP-CSOs that connect via the DISA BCAP must also have a Cloud Approval to Connect (CATC) issued by DISA.

- Information Impact Level 4 or 5 C-ITPs that connect via a DISA BCAP must also have a Cloud Permission to Connect (CPTC) issued by DISA.

- Since On-premise CSP-CSO's connect to the NIPRNet via an ICAP, they must have an Authorization to Operate (ATO) obtained pursuant to DoDI 8510.01 (ref b) and a NIPRNet Approval to Connect (ATC) obtained in accordance with the DISN CPG (ref f) A CATC is not required for an On-Premise CSP-CSO.

IAPs and CAPs may integrate with pre-existing and emerging DODIN capabilities such as the NIPRNet De-Militarized Zone (DMZ) and the Joint Regional Security Stack (JRSS) to provide an additional layer of security functionality necessary to defend against threats from using the CSP.

Service Models[7]: A cloud can provide access to software applications such as email or office productivity tools (the Software as a Service, or SaaS, service model), or can provide an environment for customers to use to build and operate their own software (the Platform as a Service, or PaaS, service model), or can provide network access to traditional computing resources such as processing power and storage (the Infrastructure as a Service, or IaaS, service model). The different service models have different strengths and are suitable for different customers and mission objectives. (ref j)

- ***Cloud Software as a Service (SaaS).*** The capability provided to the Mission Owner is to use the provider's applications running on a cloud infrastructure. The applications are accessible from various client devices through a thin client interface such as a Web browser (e.g., Web-based email), or a program interface. The Mission Owner does not manage or control the underlying cloud infrastructure including network, servers, operating systems, storage, or even individual application capabilities, with the possible exception of limited user-specific application configuration settings.

Stack (JRSS). On the other hand, an ICAP may have special capabilities to support specific missions, CSP types (commercial or DoD), or cloud services.

[7] See NIST SP 800-146, (ref j)

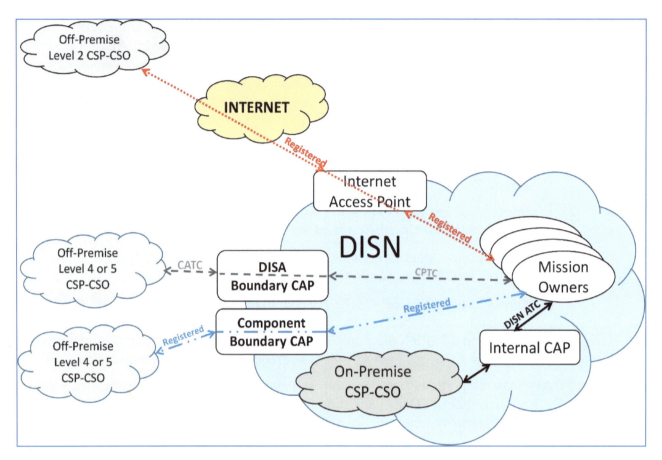

Figure 1:   On-Premise and Off-Premise CSP-CSO

- ***Cloud Platform as a Service (PaaS).*** Provides the Mission Owner the capability to deploy onto the cloud infrastructure the Mission Owner's applications created using programming languages and tools supported by the provider. The Mission Owner does not manage or control the underlying cloud infrastructure including network, servers, operating systems, or storage, but has control over the deployed applications and possibly application hosting environment configurations.

- ***Cloud Infrastructure as a Service (IaaS).*** The capability provided to the Mission Owner is to provision processing, storage, networks, and other fundamental computing resources where the Mission Owner is able to deploy and run arbitrary software, which can include operating systems and applications. The Mission Owner does not manage or control the underlying cloud infrastructure but has control over operating systems, storage, deployed applications; and possibly limited control of select networking components (e.g., host firewalls).

Third Party Assessment Organization (3PAO) A 3PAO is an independent organization accredited to help CSPs and government agencies meet FedRAMP compliance regulations. A 3PAO has demonstrated independence and technical competency required to test security implementations and collect representative evidence. The American Association for Laboratory Accreditation (A2LA) accredits FedRAMP 3PAOs with the FedRAMP PMO providing final approval.

1.7 User Connections to a CSP-CSOs

Figure 2 illustrates the connectivity and information exchanges between users and the CSP-CSOs. (Note: The below subparagraphs are color coded to match data flow in Figure 2.)

   a. Information exchanges between a user connected to the NIPRNet and a C-ITP operating in an Off-Premise Information Impact Level 4 (or 5) CSP-CSO must traverse a DoD CIO-approved BCAP.

   b. Information exchanges between a user connected to the Internet and a C-ITP operating in an Off-Premise Information Impact Level 4 or 5 CSP-CSO must traverse a DoD Internet Access Point (IAP), and a DoD CIO-approved BCAP. A Mission Owner must work with its Component Ports, Protocols, and Services Management (PPSM) Technical Advisory Group (TAG) representative (ref k) to register these connections in the NIPRNet DMZ Whitelist (ref m) to IAP enable connections through the IAP.

> A CAP does not support or provide direct Internet access to an Information Impact Level 4/5 CSP-CSO. Information exchanges between a Level 4/5 CSP-CSO and the Internet must transit both an and a CAP. Additionally, Mission Owners must register Internet-facing connections in the NIPRNet DMZ Whitelist (ref m) to enable interoperability as illustrated in Figure 2.

   c. Information exchanges between a user connected to the NIPRNet and a C-ITP operating in an Information Impact Level 2 CSP-CSO connected to the Internet must traverse a DoD IAP. Mission Owners should consult with their PPSM TAG representative (ref k) to determine if these user connections must be registered in the NIPRNet DMZ Whitelist to enable connections through the IAP (ref m).

   d. Information exchanges between a user connected to the Internet[8] and a C-ITP operating in an Information Impact Level 2 CSP-CSO connected to the Internet are direct via the Internet.

---

[8] Note: "Use of commercially provided transport as an alternative to available DISN-provided transport requires a Commercial ISP Connection Waiver IAW the DISA Connection Process Guide." - CJCSI 6211.02D online at http://www.dtic.mil/cjcs_directives/cjcs/instructions.htm

---

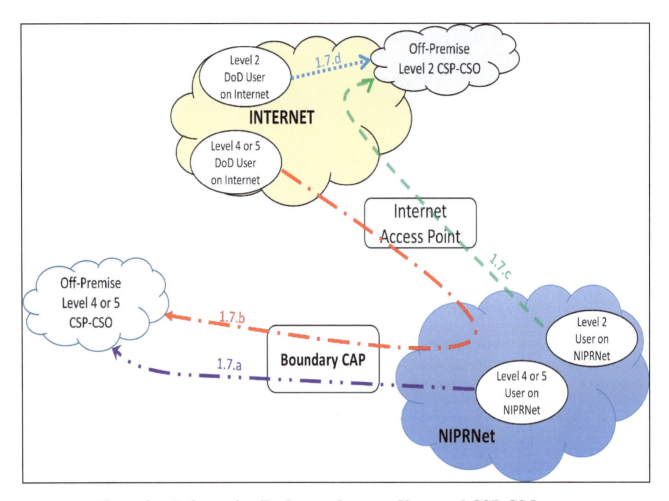

Figure 2:   Information Exchanges between Users and CSP-CSOs

1.8 Cloud Registration and Connection Processes

Figure 3 illustrates the Cloud Registration and Connection Processes addressed in this Cloud CPG. It illustrates two tracks, one for CSP-CSO connections, and another for C-ITP connections. It also illustrates the touch points between these two tracks.

Touch point #1 on the left side of the diagram, illustrates the situation in which a DoD Mission Owner wants to use a CSP-CSO that does not have the required DoD PA. In this case, the DoD Mission Owner would become the DoD Sponsor for the CSP-CSO to enter cloud connection process. Touch point #2 in the center of the diagram occurs when the CSP-CSO receives its DoD PA. The awarding of the DoD PA permits the DoD Mission Owner to register the intended use of the now-authorized CSP-CSO to host a mission C-ITP. Touch Point #3 occurs when the requirement or authorization for a connection between a CSP-CSO and a C-ITP ends. This guide addresses each of the Cloud connection processes for CSP-CSOs (Section 2) and C-ITPs (Section 3) including cloud registration and connection, connection sustainment and maintenance, and discontinuation of services at the end of the connection's life cycle.

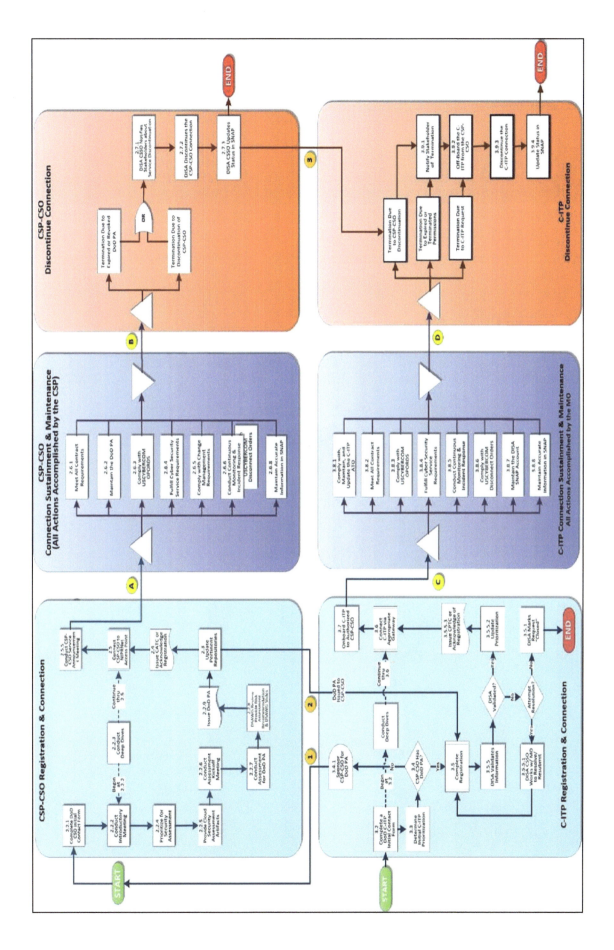

Figure 3: Cloud Registration and Connection Processes

This page intentionally left blank

SECTION 2. CLOUD SERVICE PROVIDER-CLOUD SERVICE OFFERING (CSP-CSO) REGISTRATION AND CONNECTION LIFE CYCLE

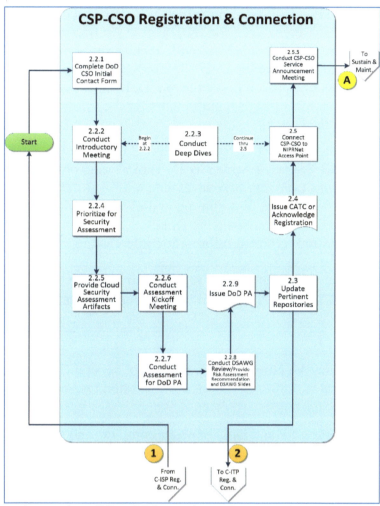

Figure 4: CSP-CSO Registration and Connection

2.1 Introduction

This section describes the Cloud registration and connection processes involved with connecting a CSP-CSO to the DISN as illustrated in Figure 4. The DoD Mission Owner/Sponsor or CSP may initiate the process. Upon successful completion, the CSP-CSO is available for use by Mission Owners using the procedures in Section 3 of this guide. Although some cloud connection processes in this section are the same for all CSP-CSOs, other processes vary depending on the authorized Information Impact Level of the CSP-CSO. The process for connecting a CSP-CSO to a DoD BCAP is a joint effort among: the CSP, DISA, the DoD Security/Cybersecurity Authorization Working Group (DSAWG), the DoD CIO (ref c) and may include a DoD Mission Owner that wishes to use a CSP-CSO), a DoD Sponsor, along with the sponsoring DoD Component's Cloud migration office. The requirements for registration and connection of a CSP-CSO to the DISN include: obtaining a DoD PA; working with DISA CSSO to register the CSP-CSO in the DISA SNAP database (ref e); connecting the CSP-CSO to the DISN via an appropriate access point; maintaining the CSP-CSO connection and DoD PA; and discontinuation of the CSP-CSO connection at the end of the life cycle.

2.2 Obtain a DoD PA for a CSP-CSO

In order to host a DoD C-ITP, a CSP-CSO must have a DoD PA and be connected to the NIPRNet via an ICAP (for On-Premise CSP-CSO), a DoD CIO-approved BCAP (Off-Premise Information Impact Level 4 or 5 CSP-CSO), or an IAP (Information Impact Level 2 CSP-CSO) as illustrated in Figure 1. Section 3 of the DoD Cloud SRG (ref d) provides guidance for determining the appropriate information impact level. DoD must assess a CSP-CSO for compliance with DoD Cloud SRG (ref d) requirements for the Information Impact Level authorization requested by the CSP.

2.2.1 Complete DoD Cloud Support Offering Initial Contact Form. The CSP and its DoD Sponsor contacts the DISA CSSO (see Appendix D, Table 7) and obtains and completes a *DoD Cloud Service Offering Initial Contact Form* accessible at (ref n). The CSP will complete and submit the form to disa.meade.re.mbx.disa-commercial-cloud@mail.mil. The DISA CSSO will help the CSP and any DoD Sponsor navigate the DoD PA, registration and connection process and schedule administrative and technical information interchange meetings.

> CSPs must work with DISA CSSO to register their Information Impact Level 2, 4, & 5 CSP-CSOs in SNAP. Information Impact Level 6 (secret) CSP-CSOs must be registered in SGS when the SGS cloud module becomes available (Appendix H).

2.2.2 Conduct Introductory Meeting. This is the first of several Cloud connection meetings among the stakeholders, that is, DISA, DoD Sponsor, Mission Owners, and the CSP. The DISA CSSO hosts this meeting.

- Prerequisites - the CSP and DoD Sponsor complete and submit Checklists and Assessment Request described above.

- Objectives - Provide stakeholders an overview of the DoD cloud registration and connection process, DoD requirements to obtain a DoD PA, the CSP's CSO capabilities, and the responsibilities of the CSP, the DoD Sponsor, Mission Owners, and DISA. Also, the DoD assessor is identified (e.g., the DISA Cloud Assessment Team or DoD Component in collaboration with the DISA Cloud Assessment Team).

2.2.3 Conduct Periodic CSP-CSO Deep Dive Meeting(s). DISA will host Deep Dive technical and/or policy centric meetings with the CSP and DoD Mission Owner/Sponsor to exchange detailed information that supports the Assessment Process and the Registration and Connection Process. Planning for engineering and provisioning the CSP-CSO connection may proceed in parallel with the DoD PA assessment.

- Prerequisites – Complete the CSP Connection Readiness Checklist; Respond to actions or data requirements from the Kick Off Meeting; and Concurrence of the DISA Cloud Assessment Team and Enterprise BCAP Team.

- Objectives – Resolve issues encountered during the FedRAMP+ assessment; Engineer and provision the CSP-CSO connection to the DISA Enterprise BCAP;

identify the Meet-Me-Point; establish the CONOPS and responsibilities; identify DoD policy compliance/deviations.

2.2.4 Prioritize for Security Assessment. The DISA Cloud Assessment Team has limited resources and will likely place a request for an Information Impact Level 4 or higher assessment in a queue based on its priority.[9] The priority classes for CSP-CSO are defined as follows.

- Top Priority: CSPs with a DoD sponsor that support a high priority DoD mission as recognized by a DoD Chief Information Officer or J6 General Officer. In the event multiple CSPs fall into this category, resolution of priorities will be determined by a designated SecDef or JCS senior.

- CSP renewing an expiring Provisional Authorization that currently host DoD IT Projects.

- CSP with a DoD sponsor with these prerequisites: (1) CSP has completed the FedRAMP process; (2) CSP has an existing contract; (3) CSP rate high on readiness checklist; (4) CSP Sponsor has an IA resource to help with the analysis of the 3PAO's assessment products.

- CSP with DoD sponsor currently operating in a DoD private cloud scenario and has a second DoD sponsor seeking its services.

- CSP with a DoD sponsor not meeting the above conditions.

- Least Priority: CSPs without a DoD sponsor but have a capability aligned to a recognized DoD interest.

2.2.5 Provide Cloud Security Assessment Artifacts. The CSP provides the documentations and artifacts listed in the *CSP Security Package Documentation Checklist* (ref o) posted at http://iase.disa.mil/cloud_security/Pages/index.aspx. Also posted at this location are templates the CSP can use to revise the CSP-CSO's System Security Plan to satisfy DoD FedRAMP+ requirements for Information Impact Levels 4 and 5.[10] Forward the required documents and artifacts to the DISA Cloud Assessment Team. See Appendix D, Table 7 for DISA Cloud Assessment Team contact information.

2.2.6 Conduct Assessment Kickoff Meeting. This meeting will signify that the CSP-CSO is entering the Assessment Phase. DISA schedules the Kickoff Meeting for an Information Impact Level 4 or higher FedRAMP+ assessment when the DoD Cloud Assessor (e.g., DISA Cloud Assessment Team or a DoD Component Assessor) is ready to begin the assessment. The DISA Cloud Assessment team hosts this meeting.

- Prerequisites - DoD Assessor is identified; Concurrence of the DISA Cloud Assessment Team; a complete and well-prepared package of assessment documents and artifacts; a CSP-CSO architecture briefing; a 3PAO Security Assessment Report

---

[9] A DoD Component has the option to apply its available resources to augment the DISA Cloud Assessment Team's FedRAMP+ assessment of a sponsored CSP-CSO. Augmenting the DISA FedRAMP+ assessment effort will help move the CSP-CSO forward in the assessment queue. There are SSP Addendum Templates that detail additional security controls required for an Information Impact Level 4 or Level 5 DoD FedRAMP+ System Security Plan. Both templates are located at: http://iase.disa.mil/cloud_security/Pages/ssp-addendum.aspx

[10] If the cited documents are not published at the indicated website, contact the DISA Cloud Assessment Team using the contact information in Appendix D, Table 7.

(SAR) briefing; a DoD Readiness Assessment Report prepared by the 3PAO. The "CSP Security Package Documentation Checklist," CSP-CSO architecture briefing template, and 3PAO SAR briefing template are available at the following website [10] http://iase.disa.mil/cloud_security/Pages/index.aspx

- Objectives – The CSP presents the architecture briefing; the 3PAO presents the SAR briefing; the participants review the assessment package for readiness; DISA presents an overview of the assessment process and establishes the timeline for the assessment.

2.2.7 Conduct Assessment for DoD PA. The DISA Cloud Assessment Team or a DoD Component Assessor conducts the assessment:

- **Impact Level 2 DoD PA Request.** A CSP-CSO that has an existing FedRAMP Joint Acquisition Board (JAB) or Federal Agency Moderate Provisional Authorizations will receive a DoD PA and DISA will list the CSP-CSO in the DoD Catalog of Approved CSP-CSOs (ref p) within 2 weeks.

- **Information Impact Level 4 or higher FedRAMP+ Assessment.** A request for an Impact Level 4, 5 or 6 DoD PA is required to undergo a DoD FedRAMP+ assessment in accordance with the criteria outlined in the DoD Cloud SRG (ref d). The DISA Cloud Assessment Team or a DoD Component assessor may perform the FedRAMP+ security assessment. The DoD Component assessor will use information provided by the CSP's certified Third Party Assessment Organization (3PAO) to produce a report to the DISA Cloud Assessment Team. The DISA Cloud Assessment Team and DoD Component assessor will make the DoD PA recommendation to the DISA AO. Information Impact Level 4 and higher assessments performed by DISA takes 12-13 weeks for a CSP-CSO with a complete and well-prepared assessment package. The FedRAMP+ assessment process validates the CSP—CSO's implementation of the security controls specified in the DoD Cloud SRG (ref d). The assessment process may use any one of three following types of PA's as a starting foundation:

  (1) CSP-CSO's with a FedRAMP Joint Acquisition Board (JAB) Moderate PA[11] or in the process of obtaining a JAB PA, or a

  (2) Provisional Authorization granted by a Federal Agency, or a

  (3) DoD Component Self-Assessed Provisional Authorization.

2.2.8 DSAWG Review. The Cloud Assessment Team collaborates with the CSP to present the CSP-CSO to the Department of Defense Security/Cybersecurity Authorization Working Group (DSAWG) after completion of the FedRAMP+ assessment. The DSAWG provides risk assessment recommendation to the DISA Authorizing Official (AO). The DoD assessor's assessment scorecard and DSAWG recommendation are factors considered by the DISA AO when determining whether to issue a DoD PA. CSPs can bring technical subject matter experts to the DSAWG meetings to assist in responding to the DSAWG member's inquiries.
The members of the DSAWG represent the Principal Authorizing Officials of the DoD Mission Areas (Warfighting, Intelligences, Business, and Enterprise Information Environment) and DoD Components. The DSAWG assesses the risk to the DODIN community related to the CSP-CSO

---

[11] In the future, DoD will also be accepting FedRAMP High Baseline PAs for DoD Level 4 PA equivalence.

connection to the DISN. The DISA Cloud Assessment Team Lead will coordinate and schedule participation in the DSAWG meetings and present on behalf of the CSP.

- Prerequisites – DISA Cloud Assessment Team recommendation, the assessment request, a presentation prepared IAW the DSAWG briefing template,[12] and the entire body of evidence/security relevant artifacts submitted prior to the DSAWG meeting.

- Objective – Obtain a DSAWG recommendation to the DISA AO

2.2.9 Issue the DoD PA. The DISA AO issues a DoD PA for the CSP-CSO following a positive recommendation by the DoD Assessor and the DSAWG. The DoD PA signifies that a CSP-CSO has met minimum-security requirements to host DoD data at the assessed information impact level. The output of this process is the signed DoD PA and the associated security documentation package.

2.3 Update Pertinent Repositories with CSP-CSO Information

Once the DISA AO issues the DoD PA, the DISA CSSO will create an entry for the CSP-CSO in the DoD Approved Cloud Service Offerings Catalog (ref p) and work with the CSP and DoD Mission Owner/Sponsor to register the CSP-CSO in DISA SNAP (ref e). The CSP must provide to DISA CSSO the applicable documentation and information listed in Appendix J under the columns labeled *CSO Registration*. DISA CSSO will enter this information into the DISA SNAP database. The DISA CSSO will continue to work with the CSP and DoD Mission Owner/Sponsor to update the CSP-CSO entry in DISA SNAP annually or as required.

2.4 Issue CATC or Acknowledgement of Registration.

After the DISA CSSO registers the CSP-CSO in DISA SNAP, the CSP-CSO will be available for selection by DoD Mission Owners and use in accordance with terms in the DoD PA. Either DISA CSSO will issue a *Cloud Approval to Connect (CATC)* or an *Acknowledgement of Registration* for a CSP-CSO as described in paragraph 2.5. Note that Section 3 of this guide describes the process used by Mission Owners to request a connection to an authorized CSP-CSO.

2.5 Connect CSP-CSO to the Appropriate Gateway

The appropriate gateway (e.g., IAP, BCAP, ICAP) used to connect the CSP-CSO to the NIPRNet will vary as illustrated in 4 and described in the subparagraphs below. DISA will work with the CSP and DoD Component Sponsor[13] and Mission Owners to engineer the appropriate connection between the CSP enclave and the NIPRNet including obtaining IP address space. CSP must coordinate with the Mission Owners and/or DISA to support the registration of the IP address ranges of all Internet facing web/application servers in the NIPRNet DMZ Whitelist (ref m). Mission Owners and/or DISA will obtain approved DoD DMZ addresses for the purpose. See the discussion of Whitelisting in the Cloud SRG (ref d).

---

[12] The DSAWG briefing template is located on the DSAWG website at https://intelshare.intelink.gov/sites/dsawg If a CSP does not have access to a Common Access Card (CAC), it may need assistance from a DoD sponsor or DISA to obtain a softcopy of the template. DSAWG meetings are held the second Tuesday of each Month.

[13] CJCSI 6211.02D, Defense Information Systems Network (DISN) Responsibilities requires that Mission Partner (including Defense Contractor) connections to the DISN be sponsored by a DoD Component.

The DISA Cloud PMO conducts engineering of the CSP-CSO connection to the NIPRNet in parallel with the assessment and registration processes. The goal is to activate the CSP-CSO connection when the assessment and registration are completed.

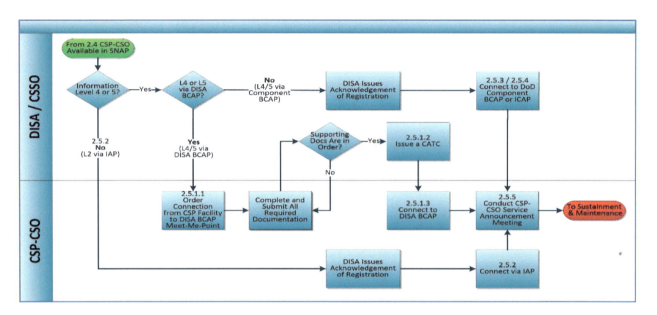

Figure 5:   Connect CSP-CSO to the Appropriate Gateway

2.5.1 Information Impact Level 4 or 5 CSP-CSO Connecting via the DISA BCAP.
Normally, all CSP-CSOs connect to the DISN via a DISA Enterprise CAP. A CSP must first obtain a DoD PA for a CSP-CSO as described in section 2.3 above, work with DISA CSSO to register the CSP-CSO in DISA SNAP. The CSP must also and obtain a DISA Cloud Approval to Connect (CATC) via a DISA BCAP as follows.

2.5.1.1 Order a Connection from the CSP-facility to the DISA BCAP Meet-Me-Point. The DISA BCAP meet-me-points are located in facilities that also host many CSP-CSOs. For those CSP-CSOs not collocated with a DISA BCAP meet-me-point, the CSP must obtain/sustain and fund a connection between CSP enclave hosting the CSP-CSO and the DISA Enterprise BCAP meet-me-point as illustrated in Figure 6.

2.5.1.2 DISA CSSO Issues a CATC. When supporting documentation and information required for a CATC (see Appendix J) is in order, the DISA CSSO will issue the CSP a Cloud Approval to Connect (CATC) for the CSP-CSO. The CSP-CSO can then be connected to a DISA Enterprise BCAP as follows.

2.5.1.3 Connection to a DISA BCAP. DISA provisions connectivity between the DISN and a DoD "Off-Premise" CSP-CSO. Information exchanges between an Information Impact Level 4 or 5 CSP-CSOs and DoD users must traverse a DoD CIO–approved BCAP. As illustrated in Figure 5, information exchanges will traverse the CSP's enclave, the connection to a Meet-Me-Point, the cross-connection via DISN transport to the DISA BCAP facility, and finally the

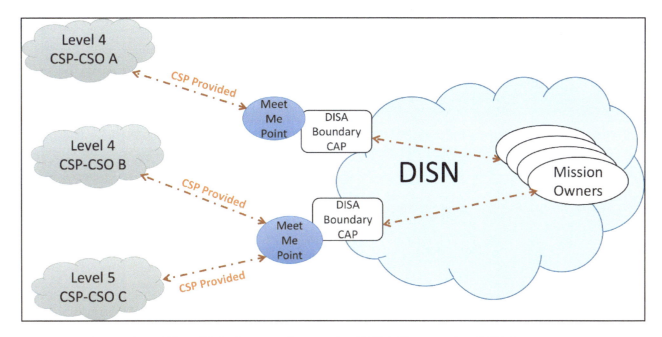

Figure 6: CSP-CSO Connection to the DISA Enterprise BCAP

connection to the DISN NIPRNet. Several stakeholders will be involved with connecting an Off-Premise CSP-CSO to the DISA Enterprise BCAP. These stakeholders are DISA, the DoD contracted transport provider, the Meet-Me-Point provider, and the CSP offering the CSP-CSO. Figure 7 illustrates the CSP-CSO connection provisioning process. At the completion of this step, the CSP-CSO is available for use and enters the Connection Sustainment and Maintenance process described in Section 2.7.

DoDI 8410.01 (ref q) requires DoD to conduct DoD public and private Internet-based communications (e.g., electronic mail and Web operations) under the "*.mil*" Top Level Domain. The DoD Cloud SRG (ref d) includes a section that stipulates requirements for Internet Protocol (IP) Addressing and Domain Name Services (DNS). Additionally, DoD IP address space is assigned by the DISA Network Information Center (NIC), the DISA Cloud PMO, and DISA CSSO can also help CSPs obtain needed IP address space. (See Appendix D, Table 7 for contact information).

2.5.2 Information Impact Level 2 CSP-CSO Connecting Via a NIPRNet Internet Access Point (IAP). Level 2 CSP-CSO's enclaves typically connect to the Internet and have connectivity to the NIPRNet via a NIPRNet IAP as illustrated in Figure 2. As such, Information Impact Level 2 CSP-CSO's are not required to have a Cloud Approval to Connect (CATC). Once the DISA CSSO registers the CSP-CSO in DISA SNAP (ref e), the CSP-CSO is immediately available for use/on-boarding by any Mission Owner wanting to host Impact Level 2 DoD C-ITP. The Mission Owner follows the process described in Section 3 of this guide for registering and connecting a C-ITP to the authorized CSP-CSO. As noted in paragraph 2.5 above, applications supported by a CSP-CSO that will be accessed by users connecting from the Internet (aka internet facing) must be registered in the NIPRNet DMZ Whitelist (ref m).

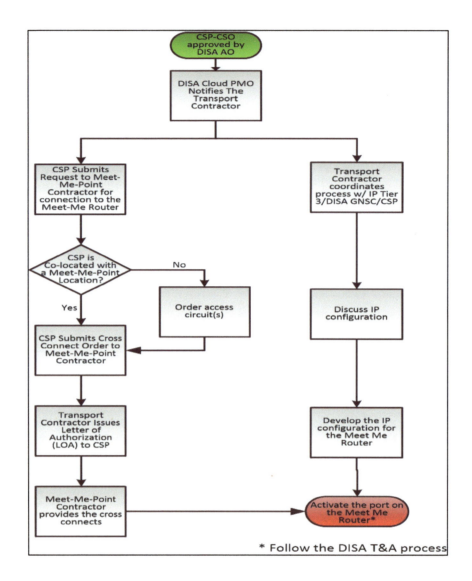

Figure 7: Provisioning the CSP-CSO Connection to the DISA Enterprise BCAP

2.5.3 Impact Level 4 or 5 CSP-CSO Connecting to the DISN via a DoD Component BCAP.
Normally all CSP-CSOs connect to the DISN via a DISA Enterprise CAP. However, CSPs have the option also to connect a CSP-CSO via a DoD CIO-approved DoD Component BCAP. Appendix B has procedures for connecting an authorized and registered Information Impact Level 4 or 5 CSP-CSO to a DoD Component BCAP. Appendix B, Table 5 identifies points of contact for Component BCAPs.

2.5.4 An On-Premise CSP-CSO Connecting Directly to the NIPRNet Via an ICAP. A CSP must obtain a DoD PA; work with DISA CSSO to register the CSP-CSO in DISA SNAP (ref e). A Cloud Approval to Connect is not required for an On-Premise CSP-CSO. Instead, an On-Premise CSP- CSO must have an Authorization to Operate (ATO) obtained in accordance with DoDI 8510.01 (ref b), and receive a NIPRNet Approval to Connect (ATC) to the NIPRNet in accordance with the DISN CPG (ref f).

In addition to obtaining a DoD PA and being registered in DISA SNAP, an <u>On-Premise</u> CSP-CSO must also obtain an Authorization to Operate in accordance with DoDI 8510.01 (ref b) and the DoD Cloud SRG (ref d) along with an Approval to Connect to the NIPRNet in accordance with the DISN CPG (ref f). ICAP cybersecurity requirements will be refined as part of the ongoing MilCloud 2 initiative.

2. 5. Conduct CSP-CSO Service Announcement Meeting. DISA conducts the CSP-CSO Service Announcement Meeting after the DISA AO issues the DoD PA. This meeting will inform the DoD Community that the CSP-CSO is available for use at the assessed information impact level. The audience includes representatives from the Component Cloud migration offices (Appendix D, Table 6), DISA Customer Engagement Group (Appendix D, Table 7) and others.

- Prerequisites: A DoD PA; DISA Service Announcement presentation; CSP's CSO presentation (CSP format), and DISA has connected the CSP-CSO to the DISN via the appropriate gateway.

- Objectives - Overview of CSP-CSO Ordering Process; Confirm the description of the CSP-CSO that DISA will post in the DoD Approved Cloud Service Offering Catalog (ref p).

2.6 CSP-CSO Connection Sustainment and Maintenance

Figure 8 illustrates the requirements for sustaining and maintaining a CSP-CSO connection to the DISN via the DISA BCAP:

2.6.1 Meet all contract requirements. The CSP and DoD Mission Owners using a CSP-CSO must meet all obligations within their contract including those specified in the Defense Federal Acquisition Regulation Supplement (DFARS): Network Penetration Reporting and Contracting for Cloud Services (DFARS Case 2013–D018) (ref r).

2.6.2 Maintain the DoD PA. CSPs must continuously monitor CSP-CSOs compliance with conditions specified in the DoD Cloud SRG (ref d) and the DoD PA for the CSP-CSO. CSPs must also submit timely renewal request prior to the expiration date when specified in the CSP-CSO's DoD PA.

2.6.3 Comply with USCYBERCOM Operational Orders (OPORDS). In the case that a USCYBERCOM OPORD affects a CSP-CSO, the Cybersecurity Services Provider and Contract Officer are responsible for providing the unclassified portion of the OPORD to the CSP and ensuring compliance. CSPs must ensure CSP-CSOs comply with applicable USCYBERCOM OPORDS.

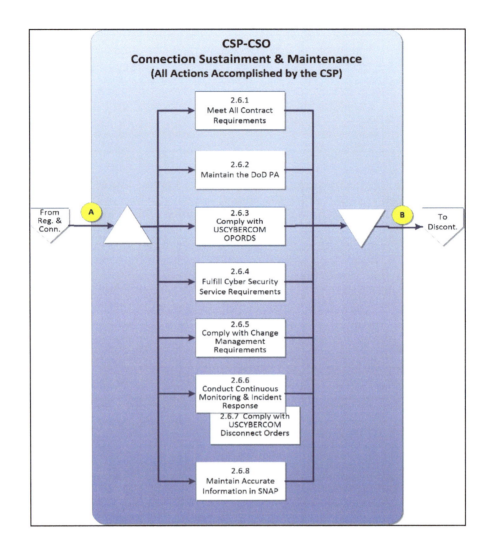

Figure 8: CSP-CSO Connection Sustainment and Maintenance Process

2.6.4 Fulfill Cyber Security Service Requirements. All CSPs and DoD Mission Owners/Sponsors are required to ensure their CSP-CSOs comply with DoD Cyber Security Service Provider (CSSP) (aka Cyber Defense Services) requirements in accordance with the DoD Cloud SRG (ref d).

2.6.5 Change Management. The CSP must submit a *FedRAMP Significant Change Security Impact Analysis Form* to the responsible 3PAO and the DISA CSSO following the procedures described in the *Change Control* section of the DoD Cloud SRG (ref d). NIST Special Publication 800-37 (ref s) defines a significant change as "a change that is likely to affect the security state of an information system.[14]" a change to the scope of an approved PA or an impact to the

---

[14] The following examples are only *significant changes* when they are likely to affect the security state of the information system: (i) installation of a new or upgraded operating system, middleware component, or application; (ii) modifications to system ports, protocols, or services; (iii) installation of a new or upgraded hardware platform; (iv) modifications to cryptographic modules or services; or (v) modifications to security controls. Examples of significant changes to the environment of operation may include for example: (i) moving to a new facility; (ii) adding new core missions or business functions; (iii) acquiring specific and credible threat information that the organization is being targeted by a threat source; or (iv) establishing new/modified laws, directives, policies, or regulations.

authorization boundary of the CSP-CSO. The DoD Cloud SRG (ref d) describes procedures for obtaining approval for significant changes to the CSP-CSO prior to the implementation. The CSP must obtain a new DoD PA from DISA for the CSP-CSO and work with the DISA CSSO to update the CSP-CSO record in the DISA SNAP database (ref e).

2.6.6 Conduct Continuous Monitoring and Incident Response.

a. Both FedRAMP and DoD require an ongoing assessment and authorization capability for CSPs providing services to the DoD described in the FedRAMP CONOPS and Continuous Monitoring Strategy Guide (ref t). The strategy addresses continuous monitoring, change control, and incident response. Continuous monitoring includes monitoring security controls employed within or inherited by the system, and monitoring of any proposed or actual changes to the system and its environment of operation in accordance with DoDI 8510.01 (ref b), and NIST SP 800-137 (ref u).

b. The DoD Cloud SRG requires that information systems (e.g., CSP-CSOs and C-ITPs) align with a CSSP to support continuous monitoring. CSPs must report cyber incidents in accordance with (ref d) and FedRAMP incident report requirements found in the FedRAMP Incident Response Requirements and Process Verification (ref v). DoD CSSPs will report all incidents in accordance with normal DoD processes using the Joint Incident Management System (JIMS) on SIPRNet.

c. DoD policy (ref b) requires CSPs and Mission Owner to configure information systems in accordance with the DoD Cloud SRG (ref d). The responsible DoD Assessor will review all significant changes planned by a CSP for a CSP-CSO to determine if a new DoD PA is required.

d. The DoD Cloud SRG (ref d) provides details about incident response processes and information exchanges, which differ depending on the origin of the CSP-CSO's authority. Commercial CSPs are encouraged to report cyber incidents involving unclassified CSP-CSOs via the on-line Defense Industrial Base (DIB) Incident Collection Format found at http://dibnet.dod.mil/ in accordance with the DFARS (ref r). Use of this on-line CSP Incident Report[15] is preferred. Access to this format requires a DoD-approved medium assurance External Certificate Authority (ECA) certificate. CSP personnel unable to access this format should call (877) 838-2174 or email DCISE@DC3.mil. The Defense Industrial Base Network (DIBNet) portal access and unclassified cybersecurity incident reporting is at http://dibnet.dod.mil/.

 Personnel should not discuss ongoing cybersecurity events or incidents using unclassified means. Use the unclassified DIBNET format to report cyber incidents at the unclassified level. Any follow-on discussions must be via appropriately secured communications channels.

---

[15] The unclassified DIBNET Cloud Service Provider Incident Report entry format is at: https://dcise.cert.org/web/guest/csp-incident-reporting

2.6.7 Comply with USCYBERCOM Disconnect Orders. Non-compliance or cyber incidents may result in a USCYBERCOM ordering DISA to disconnect temporarily the CSP-CSO service from the DISN until the CSP-CSO complies with the USCYBERCOM Task Order (TASKORD). The USCYBERCOM TASKORD) provides the conditions and procedures for reactivating a CSP-CSO connection. USCYBERCOM, DISA, DoD Mission Owners, CSP, and AO jointly assess the mission impact before USCYBERCOM orders DISA to disconnect temporarily or discontinue permanently a CSP-CSO connection to the DISN.

2.6.8 Maintain Accurate Information within SNAP. The CSP must collaborate with the DoD Sponsor and DISA CSSO to ensure the information about the CSP-CSO in DISA SNAP (ref e) is updated to reflect the accurate status of the CSP-CSO including personnel contact information.

2.7   Discontinue CSP-CSO Service

USCYBERCOM or a CSP may discontinue permanently a CSP-CSO connection as illustrated in Figure 9. Permanent discontinuation of a connection could be for several reasons:

- A CSP wishes to discontinue offering a CSP-CSO and its connection to the DISN.

- The JAB may revoke the FedRAMP PA or DISA AO may revoke the DoD PA for a particular CSP-CSO.

- The PA may expire.

- USCYBERCOM may issue a TASKORD to discontinue the CSP-CSO connection if the CSP-CSO does not comply with DoD cybersecurity requirements.

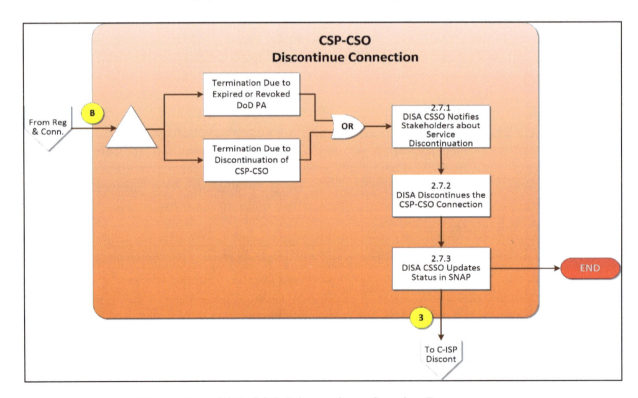

Figure 9:   CSP-CSO Discontinue Service Process

Discontinuing a CSP-CSO connection involves the following actions:

2.7.1 Notify Stakeholders about CSP-CSO Service Discontinuation. USCYBERCOM will issue an order to DISA to either temporarily disconnect or permanently discontinue the connection to the CSP-CSO. The DISA CSSO will apprise stakeholders about any discontinuation actions so they can take appropriate action (e.g., Mission Owners off-boarding C-ITP and data).

2.7.2 Discontinue the CSP-CSO Connection. DCC issues the DISA Task Order to Discontinue the CSP-CSO connection and update the NIPRNet DMZ Whitelist as needed. DISA CONUS executes the DTO and discontinues the connection to the DISN. The DISA CSSO may issue a Deny Approval to Connect (DATC) for a CSP-CSO.

2.7.3 Update Status in SNAP. The CSP in coordination with the DISA CSSO ensures DISA SNAP (ref e) entry for the CSP-CSO contains accurate information about the discontinued status of the CSP-CSO including contact information for key Points of Contact.

2.8 CSP-CSO Connection Process Checklist

The checklist in Table 1 provides the key activities the CSP must perform to obtain a connection to the DISN:

Table 1: CSP-CSO Registration and Connection Process Checklist

PROCESS STEP	IIL 4/5 via DISA BCAP	IIL2 via IAP	IIL 4/5 via Component BCAP	On-Premise via ICAP
Obtain a DoD PA for a CSP-CSO 2.2[16]	✓	✓	✓	✓
Complete the CSP-CSO Initial Contact Form (2.2.1)	✓	✓	✓	✓
Conduct Introductory Meeting (2.2.2)	✓	✓	✓	✓
Conduct Periodic CSP-CSO Deep Dive Meetings (2.2.3)	✓		✓	✓
Prioritize for Security Assessment (2.2.4)	✓	✓	✓	✓
Provide Cloud Security Assessment Artifacts (2.2.5)	✓	✓	✓	✓
Conduct Assessment Kickoff Meeting (2.2.6)	✓	✓	✓	✓
Conduct Assessment for DoD PA (2.2.7)	✓	✓	✓	✓

---

[16] On-Premise CSP-CSO will also be required to obtain an Authorization to Operate in accordance with DoDI 8510.01 (ref b)

PROCESS STEP (continued)	IIL 4/5 via DISA BCAP	IIL2 via IAP	IIL 4/5 via Component BCAP	On-Premise via ICAP
DSAWG Review (2.2.8)	✓		✓	✓
Issue the DoD PA (2.2.9)	✓	✓	✓	✓
Conduct CSP-CSO Service Announcement Meeting (2.5.5)	✓	✓	✓	✓
Update Pertinent Repositories with CSP-CSO Information (2.3)	✓	✓	✓	✓
Issue CATC or, Acknowledgement of Registration (2.4)	✓	✓	✓	✓
Connect CSPO-CSO to the Appropriate Gateway (2.5)	✓	✓	✓	✓
Information Impact Level (IIL) 4 or 5 CSP-CSO Connecting via a DISA BCAP (2.5.1)	✓			
Order a connection to the DISA BCAP Meet-Me-Point (2.5.1.1)	✓			
DISA CSSO Issues CATC (2.5.1.2)	✓			
Connection to a DISA BCAP (2.5.1.3)	✓			
IIL 2 CSP-CSO Connecting via a NIPRNet IAP (2.5.2)		✓		
IIL 4 or 5 CSP-CSO Connecting to the DISN via a DoD Component BCAP (2.5.3)			✓	
An On-Premise CSP CSO Connecting Directly to the NIPRNet via an ICAP (2.5.4)				✓
CSP-CSO Connection Sustainment and Maintenance (2.6)	✓	✓	✓	✓
Meet all Contract Requirements (2.6.1)	✓	✓	✓	✓
Maintain DoD PA (2.6.2)	✓	✓	✓	✓

PROCESS STEP (continued)	IIL 4/5 via DISA BCAP	IIL2 via IAP	IIL 4/5 via Component BCAP	On-Premise via ICAP
Comply with USCYBERCOM Operational orders (2.6.3)	✓	✓	✓	✓
Fulfill Cyber Security Service Requirements (2.6.4)	✓	✓	✓	✓
Change Management (2.6.5)	✓	✓	✓	✓
Conduct Continuous Monitoring and Incident Response (2.6.6)	✓	✓	✓	✓
Comply with USCYBERCOM Disconnect Orders (2.6.7)	✓	✓	✓	✓
Maintain Accurate information in DISA SNAP (2.6.8)	✓	✓	✓	✓
Discontinue CSP-CSO Service (2.7)	✓	✓	✓	✓
Notify Stakeholders of CSP-CSO Service Discontinuation (2.7.1)	✓	✓	✓	✓
Discontinue the CSP-CSO Connection (2.7.2)	✓	✓	✓	✓
Update Status in DISA SNAP (2.7.3)	✓	✓	✓	✓

 Information required to support a C-ITP Cloud registration and Connection Request is specified in Appendix J.

This page intentionally left blank

SECTION 3 CLOUD INFORMATION TECHNOLOGY PROJECT REGISTRATION AND CONNECTION PROCESS

3.1 Introduction Cloud Information Technology Project (C-ITP) Registration and Connection

This section addresses the process for a Mission Owner (the Cloud Consumer) to register and connect a Cloud Information Technology Project (C-ITP) to an authorized Impact Level 4 or 5 CSP-CSO via the DISA Enterprise BCAP as illustrated in the lower half of Figure 3. The process includes Registration and Connection, C-ITP on-boarding to the CSP-CSO, C-ITP sustainment and maintenance, and C-ITP discontinuation.

 Appendix B describes the procedures for connecting a C-ITP to a DoD Component BCAP. For Classified Level 6 C-ITP Connection Requests proceed to Appendix H.

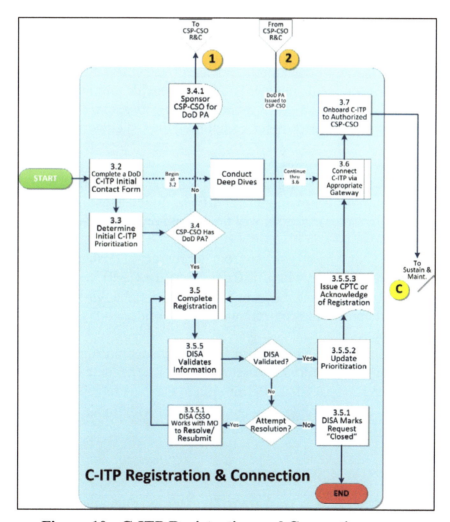

Figure 10: C-ITP Registration and Connection

As illustrated in Figure 10, each DoD Mission Owner must determine whether a C-ITP will migrate to a CSP-CSO. A DoD Component's Cloud migration office (Appendix D, Table 6) will assist its Mission Owners in the CSP-CSO selection process. The Mission Owner of a candidate C-ITP takes the following steps:

3.2 Complete a DoD Cloud IT Project Initial Contact Form

The DoD Mission Owner contacts the DISA CSSO (See Appendix D, Table 7), and obtains and completes a *DoD Cloud IT Project Initial Contact Form* accessible at (ref x). The Mission Owner will complete and submit the form to disa.meade.re.mbx.disa-commercial-cloud@mail.mil. The DISA CSSO will help the DoD Mission Owner navigate the registration and connection process and schedule administrative and technical information interchange meetings. DoDI 8410.01 (ref 17) requires DoD to conduct DoD public and private Internet-based communications (e.g., electronic mail and Web operations) under the ".*mil*" Top Level Domain. The DoD Cloud SRG (ref d) includes a section that stipulates requirements for Internet Protocol (IP) Addressing and Domain Name Services (DNS).

3.3 Determine Initial C-ITP Prioritization for Connection to a CSP-CSO.

The DISA CSSO team will evaluate the Cloud Information Technology Project's (C-ITPs) Initial Contact Form and material submitted in DISA SNAP. If the DISA Cloud team determines the C-ITP is ready for connection, the team will prioritize the request and schedule available resources for engineering the connection to the authorized CSP-CSO via the appropriate gateway. If the submission is incomplete, DISA will provide an initial prioritization that will be reassessed when the C-ITP is ready for connection (see paragraph 3.5.5.2). The following are guidelines for establishing the priority for completing the C-ITP connection to an authorized CSP-CSO:

- Top Priority: C-ITPs supporting a high priority DoD mission as recognized by a DoD chief information officer or J6 general officer. In the event multiple CSPs fall into this category, resolution of priorities will be determined by a designated SecDef or JCS senior.
- Renewing the Cloud Permission to Connect for a C-ITPs that currently hosts operational users and is due to expire within 120 days (DISA BCAP).
- C-ITPs transitioning a systems from a full operational environment (cloud or non-cloud) to a new cloud operational environment with consideration given to the Mission Owner's target date of completion.
- C-ITP has been issued a Cloud Permission to Connect in support of an operational use with consideration given to the Mission Owner's target date of completion.
- C-ITP has been issued a Cloud Permission to Connect to support a formal test event.
- Least Priority: C-ITPs conducting an assessment with no authorized plan to go operational within a 12-month window.

3.4 Determine if the CSP-CSO has a DoD PA.

3.4.1 Does the CSP-CSO have a DoD PA? The Mission Owner consults the DoD Approved Cloud Service Offerings Catalog (ref p) maintained by DISA to determine if the CSP-CSO is listed and authorized to host the IT project and its data at the required Information Impact Level.

When selecting a CSP-CSO the Mission Owner also considers the most appropriate Cloud deployment model, and the most appropriate Cloud service model. See (ref j) for details.

3.4.2 Sponsor a CSP-CSO for a DoD PA (Optional). If the selected CSP-CSO is not in the DoD Approved Cloud Service Offerings Catalog (ref p), or if the selected CSP-CSO does not have DoD PA to host the required Information Impact Level, then the Mission Owner has the option of sponsoring the CSP-CSO through the CSP-CSO Registration and Connection Process described in Section 2 of this guide.

3.5 Complete Registration of the C-ITP in DISA SNAP

DoD uses the DISA SNAP database (ref e) registration process to initiate, track, and manage Information Impact Level 2 through 5 C-ITPs in the DISA SNAP database (ref e). The DISA SNAP database provides workflow status and a place to store required documentation and artifacts. A Mission Owner must register its Information Impact Level 2, 4, and 5 (unclassified) C-ITPs in the DISA SNAP database in accordance with DoD policy (ref c). The process for registering a C-ITP's use of an authorized CSP-CSO is a joint effort by the Mission Owner, Component Cloud migration offices (Appendix D, Table 6), and DISA. The steps for a Mission Owner to request connection to an authorized CSP-CSO are:

3.5.1 Process to Obtain a DISA SNAP Account. Figure 11 illustrates steps for a Mission Owner to obtain a DISA SNAP Account:

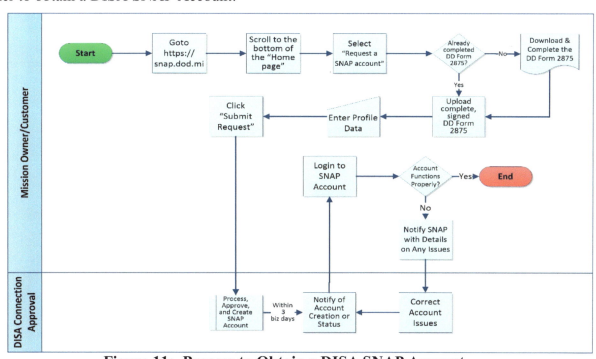

Figure 11: Process to Obtain a DISA SNAP Account

a. Go to https://snap.dod.mil for DISA SNAP (ref e).

b. Scroll to the bottom of the "Home page."

c. Select "Request a SNAP account."

d. Upload a completed signed DD Form 2875 System Authorization Access Request (SAAR). The user may download the DD Form 2875 from DISA SNAP on the *Reference Documents* webpage.

e. Complete section 13 of the DD Form 2875, "Justification for Access" by specifying the DISA SNAP and user role for your CC/S/A/ Federal Agency (FA) and request access to the:

- Mission Owner (CSP-CSO) Module,
- Virtual Private Network (VPN) Module - if a VPN connection to the NIPRNet (if required),
- NIPR Module – if a NIPRNet access circuit (if required),
- Non-DISN Connections Module.

f. Complete your profile data (note: fields in DISA SNAP with asterisks are required fields).

g. Click "Submit Request" for approval.

h. The DISA CAO will then review the submission and within three business days send an email notification whether the account request is approved or denied.

> The SNAP user guide link at the bottom on the SNAP homepage has additional instructions for entering information into SNAP modules. The *Cloud/Hosted Service Guide* is also available at https://snap.dod.mil/gcap/file/ref file.form?id=10082

3.5.2 Update SNAP and Other Pertinent Repositories with C-ITP Information. Once the Mission Owner has a DISA SNAP account, the Mission Owners will: log into the DISA SNAP database; follow the instructions in the DISA SNAP "Cloud Mission Owner" module; and provide the information and documentation indicated in Appendix J (C-ITP Registration) of this guide. Mission Owners will update other pertinent repositories (e.g., DITPR, eMASS) where appropriate. If the selected CSP-CSO is going through the DoD PA assessment process, the Mission Owner is encouraged to update the C-ITP entry in DISA SNAP as needed.

> The Mission Owner ensures the C-IPT name used in the DISA SNAP entry corresponds to the official name of the project used in the SNaP-IT and DITPR databases.

3.5.3 Submit C-ITP SNAP Package. When the Mission Owner submits all the required information, DISA SNAP will permit the Mission Owner to select the "SUBMIT" button at the bottom of the DISA SNAP screen.

3.5.4 DoD Component Reviews the Connection Request. This step only applies to DoD Component Cloud migration offices listed in Appendix D, Table 6. DISA CSSO will notify the DoD Component Cloud migration offices when one of their Component's Mission Owners submits a Cloud connection request in DISA SNAP. The responsible DoD Component Cloud migration office will indicate in DISA SNAP whether it concurs or non-concurs with a Mission Owner's Cloud connection request. If the DoD Component Cloud migration office non-concurs with the request, the Mission Owner must work with the office to resolve any issues before DISA will continue processing the cloud connection request. If issues are not resolved, DISA will mark the request as "closed" but retain any documentation loaded in DISA SNAP.

3.5.5 DISA Validates Information.

The DISA Cloud team (Table 7) reviews the Mission Owner's request for connection to an authorized CSP-CSO via the DISA Enterprise BCAP and determines whether:

- A DoD mission owner has registered connections in the NIPRNet DMZ Whitelist where appropriate (see "DoD Whitelist" in the DoD Cloud SRG (ref d)).
- DoD mission owners collaborate with their Component's PPSM TAG representative (ref k) to get ports, protocols, and services (PPS) registered in the PPSM Registry for the C-ITP located at the following SIPRNet link: https://pnp.cert.smil.mil/.
- The ports, protocols and services comply with the PPSM Category Assurance List (CAL) (ref y).[17]
- For assistance with PPSM registration, please contact your Component's PPSM Configuration Control Board (CCB) / Technical Advisory Group (TAG) representative (ref k).

3.5.5.1 DISA SNAP Package Rejection. If the CSSO cannot validate information in the connection request package, the DISA CSSO will work with the Mission Owner to resolve issues and the Mission Owner can make required changes and resubmit the package when ready. If issues are not resolved, DISA will mark the request as "closed" but will retain any documentation submitted in DISA SNAP pending further action by the Mission Owner.

3.5.5.2 DISA Validates the Cloud Connection Request and Determines Final C-ITP Prioritization. If DISA CSSO validates all information submitted by the Mission Owner, then DISA CSSO reassesses the priority of the C-ITP for connection to an authorized CSP-CSO using the guidelines described in paragraph 3.3.

3.5.5.3 DISA Issues a Cloud Permission to Connect (CPTC) or Acknowledgement of Registration. DISA CSSO will issue either a CPTC for a C-ITP connecting via a DISA BCAP or an "Acknowledgement of Registration" as described in paragraph 3.6.

---

[17] For more information on PPSM, please refer to the DISA RE4 PPSM home page at https://disa.deps.mil/org/RE4/RE42/PPSM/default.aspx, the DISA IASE PPSM page at http://iase.disa.mil/ppsm/Pages/index.aspx - or call the PPSM team (Appendix D, Table 7)

3.6 Connect the C-ITP to an Authorized CSP-CSO Via an Appropriate Gateway

Once registered in the DISA SNAP database (ref e), DISA will work with the CSP and Mission Owner to provision the connection between the C-ITP and the authorized CSP-CSO. The next steps to provision the connection depend on the Impact Level of the C-ITP and the Cloud access point the Mission Owner will use to connect to the CSP-CSO as illustrated in figure 12.

> The DISA Cloud PMO conducts engineering of the C-ITP connection in parallel with the registration process. The goal is to activate the C-ITP connection when all registration requirements are met.

3.6.1 Information Impact Level 4 or 5 C-ITP connecting via a DISA Enterprise BCAP – A CPTC is Required. In this case, the Mission Owner must obtain a Cloud Permission to Connect (CPTC) to and authorized CSP-CSO via the DISA BCAP as follows.

3.6.1.1 Order a Circuit or VPN to the DISA BCAP (if required). The Mission Owner may determine that a C-ITP requires a dedicated circuit or logical connection (e.g., VPN) to the DISA BCAP. If so, the Mission Owner may use the DISA Direct Store Front (DDSF) (ref z) to obtain the connection. The process involves the ordering, engineering, acquisition, installation of the circuit and equipment necessary to connect to the DISN. The DISN Connection Process Guide (ref f)[18] documents the step-by-step DISN connection process.

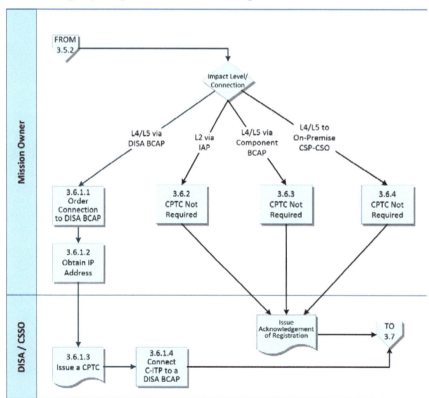

Figure 12: Connect the C-ITP to an Authorized CSP-CSO Via the Appropriate Gateway

---

[18] The DISA Connection Approval Office can be reached at: 301-225-2900/2901 or DSN 312-375-2900/2901 or disa.meade.ns.mbx.ucao@mail.mil

3.6.1.2 Obtain IP Addresses. The Mission Owner is responsible for obtaining required IP addresses. Contact the NIC, DISA CSSO (Appendix D, Table 7), or DoD Component Cloud migration office (Appendix D, Table 6) for guidance to obtain needed IP addresses. The NIC has allocated IP address space for several Cloud Service Offerings to DoD Component offices. The DoD Component points of contact assigned IP address space for CSOs and can be identified on the NIC website as follows:

a. Log into https://www.nic.mil.

b. Select "Whois Search."

c. Type in: **CLOUD***.

d. Under the column labeled "Network Name" find the desired CSP-CSO aligned with your DoD Component (e.g., "CCSNET-AF-SAAS-ORACLE," "CSSNET-ARMY-IAAS-AMAZON").

e. Double click on the associated "handle" to identify the Component POC to contact for additional direction.

If none of the listed Network Names support your requirement there are several possible ways to obtain IP-address space. Contact the DISA CSSO for additional guidance (see Appendix D, Table 7).

3.6.1.3 DISA Issues a CPTC. When supporting documentation and information required for a CPTC (see Appendix J) is in order, the DISA CSSO will issue the Mission Owner a Cloud Permission to connect (CPTC) for the C-ITP.

3.6.1.4 Connect the C-ITP to a DISA BCAP. As stated above, the DISA Cloud PMO works in parallel with the registration process to engineer the connection of an Information Impact Level 4 or 5 C-ITP to a DISA BCAP. The goal is to activate the connection when DISA issues the CPTC for the C-ITP.

3.6.2 Information Impact Level 2 C-ITP Connecting to a CSP-CSO Via an IAP –CPTC Not Required. Since the connection to an Information Impact Level 2 CSP-CSO does not involve a DoD CIO-approved CAP, the Mission Owner is not required to obtain a CPTC. Instead, the DISA CSSO will issue an "Acknowledgement of Registration" to the Mission Owner. The Mission Owner may contact the CSP to commence implementation of the C-ITP using the selected CSP-CSO in coordination with its DoD Component Cloud migration office (Appendix D, Table 6). Since an Information Impact Level 2 CSP-CSO is typically connected to the Internet, Mission Owners need to work with their PPSM TAG representative (ref l) to determine if the user connections must be registered in the NIPRNet DMZ Whitelist to enable connections through the IAP (ref m).

3.6.3 Information Impact Level 4 or 5 C-ITP Connecting to a CSP-CSO Via a DoD Component BCAP –CPTC Not Required. Normally all Level 4 or 5 CSP-CSOs connect to the DISN via a DISA Enterprise CAP. However, CSPs have the option also to connect a CSP-CSO to a DoD CIO-approved Component BCAP. A Mission Owner is not required to obtain a CPTC from DISA for a connection to a DoD Component BCAP. Instead, the DISA CSSO will issue an "Acknowledgement of Registration" to the Mission Owner. Proceed to Appendix B which for information about on-boarding a Level 4 or 5 C-ITP to a CSP-CSO via a DoD Component BCAP.

3.6.4 A C-ITP connecting to an On-Premise Impact Level 4 or 5 CSP-CSO – CPTC Not Required. An On-Premise CSP-CSO that connects directly to the DISN (e.g., MILCLOUD) does not connect via a DoD CIO-approved BCAP (see Figure 1). As a result, The Mission Owner is not required to obtain a CPTC. Instead, the DISA CSSO will issue an "Acknowledgement of Registration" to the Mission Owner and the Mission Owner may contact the CSP to commence implementation of the C-ITP using the selected CSP-CSO in coordination with its DoD Component Cloud migration office (Appendix D, Table 6).

3.7 On-board the C-ITP to an Authorized CSP-CSO

3.7.1 Best Practices Guide For DoD Cloud Mission Owners. After the DISA configures the BCAP to make the CSP-CSO accessible to users, a Mission Owner may then work with the CSP to complete activities necessary to on-board a C-ITP onto the authorized CSP-CSO. DISA wrote the *Best Practices Guide for Department of Defense Cloud Mission Owners* (ref aa) for DoD Mission Owners who are planning to migrate (or on-board) an existing information system from a physical environment to a virtualized cloud environment. The guide is not DoD policy. Instead, it is a collection of best practices discovered during the DoD CIO Cloud Pilot efforts and documented for the benefit of the DoD Community. At the completion of this step, the C-ITP enters the Connection Sustainment and Maintenance phase described in Section 3.10.

3.7.2 DoD Cloud Computing Standards. Interoperability and portability are critical to the success of DoD cloud computing. A common set of open standards to support cloud computing services provides the greatest opportunity for collaboration across the enterprise. The DoD and Intelligence Community Joint Enterprise Standards Committee (JESC) approved a set of cloud standards as "Mandated" cloud standards to promote interoperability and portability among the different clouds. The DoD IT Standards Registry (DISR) lists these mandated standards.

Table 2 is a summary of JESC approved "Mandated" Cloud Standards as of the date of this document. These standards will also serve as a guide to external clouds (e.g., Public, Partners, other USG agencies) when they are considering consuming or providing services to the JIE.

3.7.3 Open Cloud Computing Interface (OCCI) Standards. Interoperability and portability are critical to the success of DoD cloud computing. A common set of open standards to support cloud computing services provides the greatest opportunity for collaboration across the enterprise. The DoD-Intelligence Committee Joint Enterprise Standards Committee (JESC) approved two Open Cloud Computing Interface (OCCI) cloud standards OGF GFD-P-R.183 (ref bb) and OGF GFD-P-R.185 (ref cc). The JESC has mandated these two and other Cloud standards now included in the DoD IT Standards Registry (DISR)[19] as "Mandated" cloud standards to promote interoperability and portability among the different clouds. These standards will also serve as a guide to external clouds (e.g., Public, Partners, other USG agencies) when they are considering consuming or providing services to the JIE. The U.S. Army, Navy, and Air Force are adopting these standards - see:

---

[19] The DoD IT Standards Registry (DISR) is located at: https://gtg.csd.disa.mil/disr/

a. Army Enterprise Cloud Computing Reference Architecture (AECCRA) Version 1.0, September 2014.[20]

b. Army Standards Profile Guidance in support of Common Operating Environment (COE) v3, August 2014.[21]

c. Navy Cloud Security, Portability, Interoperability, Mobility Standards Profile Version 1.1, September 2013.[22]

d. Air Force Integrated Personnel and Pay System, September 2012.

e. Joint Command and Control (C2) Standards Profile/Technical Positions v.3.0.4.

Table 2: DoD Mandated Cloud Computing Standards[23]

Standard Identifier	Standard Title	Standard Class	DoD Status
ISO/IEC 17203:2011	Information technology -- Open Virtualization Format (OVF) specification, 2011-11-21	DISR	Mandated
ISO/IEC 17826:2012	Information technology -- Cloud Data Management Interface (CDMI), 2012-11-15	DISR	Mandated
GFD-P-R.183	Open Cloud Computing Interface (OCCI)- Core, Open Grid Forum, Grid Final Document 183, June 21,2011	DISR	Mandated
GFD-P-R.184	Open Cloud Computing Interface (OCCI) - RESTful HTTP Rendering, Open Grid Forum (OGF), Grid Final Document, June 21, 2011	DISR	Mandated
OGF-FGD-P-R.185	Open Cloud Computing Interface (OCCI) – RESTful HTTP Rendering, Open Grid Forum (OGF), Grid Final Document, June 21, 2011	DISR	Mandated

---

[20]See: http://ciog6.army.mil/Portals/1/Architecture/2014/20140929-US_Army_Enterprise_Cloud_Computing_Reference_Architecture_V1-0.pdf

[21]See: http://ciog6.army.mil/Portals/1/Architecture/2015/20140815-Appendix_C-Army_Standards_Profile_Guidance_in_Support_of_COE_v3.pdf

[22] See: http://www.doncio.navy.mil/TagResults.aspx?ID=104

[23] These standards are listed in the DoD IT Standards Registry (DISR)-at https://gtg.csd.disa.mil/disr/standards/search/simple.html?searchText=cloud&baseline=&status=120&intelStatus=&search=Search

3.8 C-ITP Connection Sustainment and Maintenance Process

Figure 13 illustrates the requirements for sustaining and maintaining a C-ITP connection to a CSP-CSO:

3.8.1 Comply With, Maintain, and Update the C-ITP ATO. Mission Owners must continuously monitor compliance with conditions specified in the DoD Cloud SRG (ref d), ATO, and CPTC for the C-ITP. The Mission Owner must also submit timely renewal request prior to the expiration date when specified in the C-ITP ATO and/or CPTC.

3.8.2 Meet all contract requirements. The CSP and DoD Mission Owners using a CSP-CSO must meet all obligations within their contact including those specified in the DFARS (ref r).

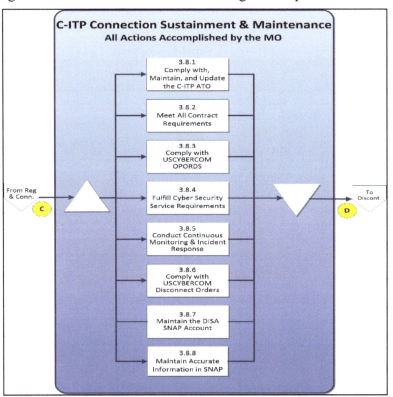

Figure 13: C-ITP Connection Sustainment and Maintenance Process

3.8.3 Comply with USCYBERCOM Operational Orders (OPORDS). Mission Owners must maintain awareness of USCYBERCOM OPORDS and directives issued via SIPRNet have personnel cleared for access to OPORDS that may be classified, and ensure the C-ITP complies with applicable USCYBERCOM OPORDS.

3.8.4 Fulfill Cybersecurity Service Requirements. DoD Sponsors are required to ensure their CSP-CSO, and C-ITPs comply with DoD Cyber Security Service Provider requirements in accordance with the DoD Cloud SRG (ref d) and annual re-assessment requirements described in DoD Cybersecurity Policy and STIGS. If the Mission Owner intends to make changes to an approved C-ITP configuration that will alter the security posture of the C-ITP, then the Mission Owner must first:

    a. Document and submit the change request to DISA CSSO using a Security Impact Analysis Form described in the DoD Cloud SRG (ref d).

    b. Obtain approval from the appropriate configuration change authority prior to the alteration.

    c. Update applicable entries in the DISA SNAP database for the C-ITP.

    d. Obtain new CPTC from the DISA CSSO.

> Cybersecurity events or incidents should not be discussed using unclassified means but use appropriately secured communications channels.

3.8.5 Conduct Continuous Monitoring and Incident Response.

    a. Both FedRAMP and DoD require an ongoing assessment and authorization capability for C-ITPs. This capability builds upon the DoD RMF and the foundation of the FedRAMP continuous monitoring strategy, as described in the FedRAMP CONOPS and Continuous Monitoring Strategy Guide (ref t). These ongoing assessment processes include continuous monitoring and change control. Continuous monitoring includes monitoring security controls and monitoring associated with Cyber Security Services. The DoD will review all significant changes planned for CSP-CSOs and a mission owner's C-ITP. The DoD Cloud SRG (ref d) provides additional details on incident response.

    b. DoD policy (ref b) requires a Mission Owner to align a C-ITP with a CSSP. Mission Owners must report cyber incidents in accordance with (ref d) and FedRAMP incident report requirements found in the FedRAMP Incident Response Requirements and Process Verification (ref v). DoD CSSPs will report all incidents in accordance with normal DoD processes using the Joint Incident Management System (JIMS) on SIPRNet.

3.8.6 Comply with USCYBERCOM Disconnect Orders.
Non-compliance or cyber incidents may result in a USCYBERCOM ordering DISA to disconnect temporarily the C-ITP from the DISN until the C-ITP or the hosting CSP-CSO comply with cloud connection requirements. The USCYBERCOM TASKORD will provide the conditions and procedures for restoring the C-ITP. USCYBERCOM, DISA, DoD Mission Owners, CSP, and AO will jointly assess the impact of any proposed disconnection to determine potential mission impacts before ordering DISA to disconnect temporarily or discontinue permanently a C-ITP connection to a CSP-CSO.

Table 3: Mission Cyberspace Defense Service Provider Contacts

Mission Cyberspace Defense (MCD) Service Provider	Provider Contact Information
DISA CSSP Office (For DISA and DoD Component C-ITPs)[24]	Unclassified Email: disa.letterkenny.re.list.cdsp-requests@mail.mil
Joint Service Provider (JSP) Pentagon (For C-ITPs using the JSP-AWS GovCloud)	Your organization's JSP Customer Account Manager or the JSP Service Desk at: Unclassified Email: EITSDCustServices@osd.mil, Phone: 703-571-4577
Other DoD Component CSSPs	DISA CSSP office (Appendix D, Table 7) maintains a list of accredited CSSPs.

3.8.7 Maintain the DISA SNAP Account. DISA SNAP users must annually submit their certificate of completion for the DoD Annual Cybersecurity Awareness Training to the DISA Connection Approval Office (See Appendix D, Table 7) for their DISA SNAP accounts to remain active.

3.8.8 Maintain Accurate Information within DISA SNAP. The Mission Owner must ensure the information about the C-ITP in DISA SNAP is updated to reflect the current, accurate, and complete status of the C-ITP including personnel contact information.

3.9 Discontinue C-ITP Service.

The proper management of the end of life (i.e., discontinuation or decommissioning) of a C-ITP is as important as the initial implementation. As illustrated in Figure 14, a Mission Owner or USCYBERCOM may discontinue permanently a C-ITP for several reasons:

- A CSP wishes to discontinue offering a CSP-CSO and its connection to the DISN.
- A Mission Owner decides to discontinue use of a CSP-CSO to host a C-ITP.
- The FedRAMP PA or DoD PA for a particular CSP-CSO is expired or revoked. The DISA AO may revoke the DoD PA for a C-ITP based on the recommendations of a DoD assessor or the DSAWG based on non-compliance with DoD Cloud policy.

Discontinuing a C-ITP involves the following actions:

3.9.1 Notify Stakeholder about C-ITP Service Termination. USCYBERCOM will issue an order to DISA to either temporarily disconnect or permanently discontinue the connection to the C-ITP. The DISA CSSO will keep stakeholders apprised of any proposals or actions that may affect the C-ITP connection to a CSP-CSO.

---

[24] DISA provides Mission Cloud Cyberspace Defense services to DoD Components on a fee-for-service basis in accordance with DoDI 8530.01 at http://www.dtic.mil/whs/directives/corres/ins1.html

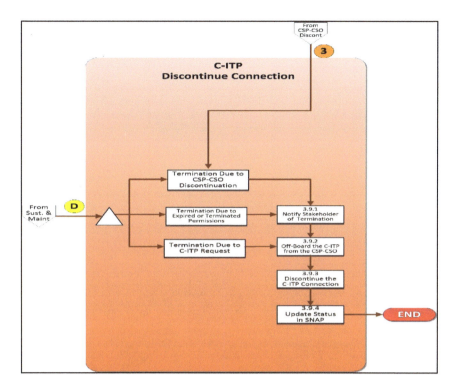

Figure 14: C-ITP Discontinue Service

3.9.2 Off-Board the C-ITP from the CSP-CSO. C-ITP discontinuation and off-boarding specifications and requirements must be included in contracts or service level agreements with CSPs in accordance with the DFARS (ref r). Mission owners must prepare for an eventual CSO off-boarding, and CSPs must support the capability in a timely manner. The off-boarding process is split into two stages: data retrieval/migration, data sanitization or destruction,[25] as well as plans for the reuse and disposal of storage media, software, and hardware. It should be a standard practice to release resources as quickly as possible, and to test the processes.

3.9.3 Discontinue the C-ITP connection. DCC issues a DISA Task Order to discontinue the C-ITP connection. DISA CONUS executes the DTO and discontinues the connection. The DISA CSSO may issue a Deny Cloud Permission To Connect (DCPTC) for the C-ITP. DISA CSSO will notify the DSAWG and/or USCYBERCOM upon completion of discontinue orders.

3.9.4 Update Status in SNAP. The Mission Owner ensures DISA SNAP entry for the C-ITP contains accurate information about the discontinued status of the C-ITPs connection including contact information for key Points of Contact.

3.10 C-ITP Registration and Connection Process Checklist

Table 4 summarizes the key activities a Mission Owner must perform to register and connect a C-ITP.

---

[25] The DoD Cloud SRG (ref d) section 5.11 *Encryption of Data-at-Rest in Commercial Cloud Storage* provides guidance on encryption of data at rest in a Cloud environment. Data-at-rest encryption, coupled with exclusive customer control of cryptographic key management, provides DoD the ability to erase data-at-rest cryptographically without CSP assistance or cooperation.

Table 4: C-ITP Registration and Connection Process Checklist

PROCESS STEP	C-ITP Connecting via a DISA BCAP (IIL 4 or 5)	C-ITP Connecting Via an IAP (IIL 2)	C-ITP Connecting via a Component BCAP (IIL 4 or 5)	C-ITP Connecting via an ICAP (On-Premise)
Complete a DoD Cloud IT Project Initial contact Form (3.2)	✓	✓	✓	✓
Determine Initial C-ITP Prioritization for Connection to a CSP-CSO (3.3)	✓	✓	✓	✓
Determine if CSP-CSO has a DoD PA (3.4)	✓	✓	✓	✓
Sponsor a CSP-CSO for a DoD PA (Optional) (3.4.1)	✓	✓	✓	✓
Complete Registration of the C-ITP in SNAP (3.5)	✓	✓	✓	✓
Obtain a DISA SNAP account (3.5.1)	✓	✓	✓	✓
Update SNAP and Other Pertinent Repositories with C-ITP Information (3.5.2)	✓	✓	✓	✓
Submit C-ITP SNAP package (3.5.3)	✓	✓	✓	✓
DoD Component Reviews the Connection Request (3.5.4) (Only applies to Components Listed in Appendix D, Table 6)	✓	✓	✓	✓
DISA Validates Information (3.5.5)	✓	✓	✓	✓
DISA Issues a *CPTC* or *Acknowledgement of Registration* (3.5.5.3)	✓	✓	✓	✓
Connect the C-ITP to an Authorized CSP-CSO Via an Appropriate Gateway (3.6)	✓	✓	✓	✓

PROCESS STEP (continued)	C-ITP Connecting via a DISA BCAP (IIL 4 or 5)	C-ITP Connecting Via an IAP (IIL 2)	C-ITP Connecting via a Component BCAP (IIL 4 or 5)	C-ITP Connecting via an ICAP (On-Premise)
IIL 4 or 5 C-ITP Connecting Via a DISA BCAP (CPTC required) (3.6.1)	✓			
Order a Circuit/VPN to DISA BCAP–if required (3.6.1.1)	✓			
Obtain IP Addresses (3.6.1.2)	✓			
DISA Issues CPTC (3.6.1.3)	✓			
Connect the C-ITP to a DISA BCAP (3.6.1.4)	✓			
IIL 2 C-ITP Connecting to a CSP-CSO VIA an IAP (CPTC is not required) (3.6.2)		✓		
IIL 4 or 5 C-ITP Connecting to a CSP-CSO via DoD Component BCAP (CPTC is not required) (3.6.3)			✓	
C-ITP Connecting to an On-Premise CSP-CSO (CPTC Not Required) (3.6.4)				✓
On-board the C-ITP to an Authorized CSP-CSO (3.7)	✓	✓	✓	✓
C-ITP Connection Sustainment and Maintenance (3.8)	✓	✓	✓	✓
Comply with, Maintain, and Update the C-ITP ATO (3.8.1)	✓	✓	✓	✓
Meet all contract requirements (3.8.2)	✓	✓	✓	✓
Comply with USCYBERCOM Operational Orders (3.8.3)	✓	✓	✓	✓
Fulfill Cybersecurity service requirements (3.8.4)	✓	✓	✓	✓

PROCESS STEP (continued)	C-ITP Connecting via a DISA BCAP (IIL 4 or 5)	C-ITP Connecting Via an IAP (IIL 2)	C-ITP Connecting via a Component BCAP (IIL 4 or 5)	C-ITP Connecting via an ICAP (On-Premise)
Conduct Continuous Monitoring and Incident Response (3.8.5)	✓	✓	✓	✓
Comply with USCYBERCOM Disconnect Orders (3.8.6)	✓	✓	✓	✓
Maintain DISA SNAP Account (3.8.7)	✓	✓	✓	✓
Maintain Accurate Information within DISA SNAP (3.8.8)	✓	✓	✓	✓
Discontinue C-ITP Service (3.9)	✓	✓	✓	✓
Notify Stakeholders about C-ITP Service Interruption (3.9.1)	✓	✓	✓	✓
Off-Board the C-ITP from the CSP-CSO (3.9.2)	✓	✓	✓	✓
Discontinue C-ITP Connection (3.9.3)	✓	✓	✓	✓
Update Status in DISA SNAP (3.9.4)	✓	✓	✓	✓

 Information required to support a C-ITP Cloud registration and Connection Request is specified in Appendix J.

APPENDIX A: REFERENCES

a. Department of Defense, DoDI 8500.01 Cybersecurity, 14 March 2014,
   [Online] http://www.dtic.mil/whs/directives/corres/ins1.html

b. Department of Defense, DoDI 8510.01 Risk Management Framework (RMF) for DoD
   Information Technology (IT), 12 March 2014
   [Online] http://www.dtic.mil/whs/directives/corres/ins1.html

c. DoD CIO Memorandum, Updated Guidance on the Acquisition and Use of Commercial
   Cloud Computing Services, 15 December 2014.

d. DoD Cloud Computing Security Requirements Guide (SRG) Version 1, Release 2, 25 March
   2016. [Online] http://iase.disa.mil/cloud_security/Pages/index.aspx

e. System Network Approval Process (SNAP) [Online] https://snap.dod.mil/index.do

f. Defense Information Systems Agency, Defense Information Systems Network (DISN)
   Connection Process Guide
   [Online] http://www.disa.mil/network-services/enterprise-connections

g. DoD CIO, Cloud Computing Strategy, July 2012.

h. U.S. CIO, Federal Risk Authorization and Management Program,
   [Online] https://www.fedramp.gov

i. DISA Risk Management Office, Cloud Access Point (CAP) Security Functional
   Requirements Document (FRD) V1.7, 2April 2015 [Online]
   https://disa.deps.mil/disa/applications/ESPortal/EntResAna/RAO/Project%20Documents/Clo
   ud%20Access%20Point%20(CAP)%20-%2033/CAP%20FRD%20draft%2004-10-
   2015%20v1.6.pdf

j. NIST Special Publication 800-146, *Cloud Computing Synopsis and Recommendations*, May
   2012 [Online] http://nvlpubs.nist.gov/nistpubs/Legacy/SP/nistspecialpublication800-146.pdf

k. DoD *Secure Cloud Computing Architecture Functional Requirements (FR), tbd*
   http://iase.disa.mil/cloud_security/Pages/index.aspx

l. PPSM Technical Advisory Group Representatives. [Online]
   https://disa.deps.mil/ext/cop/iase/ppsm/Documents/contacts_list_poc_current.pdf

m. NIPRNet DMZ Whitelist. The NIPRNet DMZ Whitelist is **on SIPRNet at**:
   https://niprdmzwhitelist.csd.disa.smil.mil/whitelist.aspx

n. DoD Cloud Service Offering (CSO) Initial Contact Form [Online]
   https://disa.deps.mil/ext/CloudServicesSupport/Cloud%20Form%20Repository/Forms/AllIte
   ms.aspx

o. CSP Security Package Documentation Checklist
   [Online] http://iase.disa.mil/cloud_security/Pages/index.aspx

p. DoD Approved Cloud Service Offerings Catalog [Online]
   https://disa.deps.mil/ext/CloudServicesSupport/Lists/TestCatalog1/AllItems.aspx

q. DoDI 8410.01, *Internet Domain Name Use and Approval*, 4 December, 2015
   http://www.dtic.mil/whs/directives/corres/pdf/841001p.pdf

r. 80 FR 51739 - Defense Federal Acquisition Regulation Supplement: Network Penetration Reporting and Contracting for Cloud Services (DFARS Case 2013-D018), August 26.2015 [Online] https://www.gpo.gov/fdsys/pkg/FR-2015-08-26/pdf/2015-20870.pdf

s. NIST Special Publication 800-37 *Guide for Applying the Risk Management Framework to Federal Information Systems: A Security Life Cycle Approach, Revision 1* [Online] http://nvlpubs.nist.gov/nistpubs/SpecialPublications/NIST.SP.800-37r1.pdf

t. 20 FedRAMP Continuous Monitoring Strategy Guide:
   [Online] https://www.fedramp.gov/resources/documents/

u. 21 NIST Special Publication 800-137, *Information Security Continuous Monitoring for Federal Information Systems and Organizations*, September 2011 [Online] http://nvlpubs.nist.gov/nistpubs/Legacy/SP/nistspecialpublication800-137.pdf

v. FedRAMP Incident Response Requirements and Process Verification [Online] https://www.fedramp.gov/provide-public-comment/incident-response-requirements-and-process-verification/

w. DoD CIO Memo, Use of Enterprise Information Technology Standard Business Case Analysis, October 23, 2014.

x. DISA CSSO, DoD Cloud IT Project Initial Contact Form, [Online] https://disa.deps.mil/ext/CloudServicesSupport/Cloud%20Form%20Repository/Forms/AllItems.aspx

y. PPSM Category Assurance List (CAL).
   [Online] https://disa.deps.mil/org/RE4/RE42/PPSM/External/Forms/AllItems.aspx?RootFol

z. DISA Direct Store Front (DDSF)
   [Online] https://disa-storefront.disa.mil/dsf/logon?a=DDR&r=https%3A%2F%2Fddsf.disadirect.disa.mil%2Fkinetic%2FDisplayPage%3Fname%3DDDSF_Home

aa. Best Practices Guide for Department of Defense Cloud Mission Owners Version 1.0 [Online] http://iasecontent.disa.mil/stigs/pdf/unclass-best_practices_guide_for_dod_cloud_mission_owners_FINAL.pdf

bb. Open Grid Forum, Open Cloud Computing Interface – Core, April 7, 2011, [Online] https://www.ogf.org/documents/GFD.183.pdf

cc. Open Grid Forum, Open Cloud Computing Interface – RESTful HTTP Rendering, June 21, 2011, [Online] https://www.ogf.org/documents/GFD.185.pdf

dd. Committee of National Security Systems Instruction (CNSSI) No. 4009, National Information Assurance (IA) Glossary, 26 April 2010. [Online] https://www.cnss.gov

ee. NIST SP 800-145, The NIST Definition of Cloud Computing, September 2011 [Online] http://dx.doi.org/10.6028/NIST.SP.800-145

ff. DoDI 8551.01, Ports, Protocols, and Services Management (PPSM), May 28, 2014 [Online] http://www.dtic.mil/whs/directives/corres/ins1.html

gg. DoD Information Technology Program Repository (DITPR).
[Online] https://ditpr.dod.mil

hh. Department of Defense, DoDI 8530.01, Cybersecurity Activities Support to DoD
Information Network Operations, March 7, 2016
[Online] http://www.dtic.mil/whs/directives/corres/ins1.html

This page intentionally left blank

APPENDIX B: PROCEDURES FOR CONNECTING A CSP-CSO TO A DoD COMPONENT BCAP

B.1 Prerequisites for an Information Impact Level 4 or 5 CSP-CSO to connect to a DoD CIO-approved DoD Component BCAP are:

- A DoD Mission Owner sponsors the CSP-CSO

- DISA has provided a DoD PA for the CSP-CSO

- The CSP and DISA CSSO have registered the CSP-CSO in DISA SNAP

- The CSP acquired a telecommunications connection from the CSP enclave to the DoD Component BCAP facility if required.

B.2 Prerequisites for an Information Impact Level 4 or 5 DoD C-ITP to connect to an Impact Level 4 or 5 CSP-CSO via a DoD CIO-approved Component BCAP.

- The CSP-CSO has a DoD PA for the appropriate Information Impact Level and is in the DoD Catalog of Approved CSP-CSO

- The C-ITP has an ATO issued by the C-ITP AO

- The Mission Owner registered the C-ITP in the DISA SNAP Database

- If required, the Mission Owner acquired a telecommunications connection (e.g., circuit, VPN) from the Mission Owner's enclave to the DoD Component BCAP facility.

B.3 Contact the following Component Cloud migration offices (Appendix D, Table 6) for procedures to on-board a C-ITP, or to connect a CSP-CSO that has a DoD (PA), to a DoD CIO-approved Component (non-DISN) BCAP.

Table 5: DoD CIO-Approved Component Cloud BCAP Points of Contact

COMPONENT	POINT OF CONTACT	CONTACT INFORMATION
Department of the Navy[26]	Commercial Hosting Lead Data Center Application Optimization (DCAO)|PEO EIS	Unclassified Email: Spawar-dcao-esm.FCM@navy.mil

---

[26] As of the publication date of this guide, only the Navy operates a DoD CIO-Approved DoD Component BCAP

This page intentionally left blank

APPENDIX C: EXCEPTIONS TO COMMERCIAL CLOUD POLICY

C.1. Overview. The DoD CIO is developing guidance for approving or denying requests for exceptions to commercial cloud policy (ref c).

C.2. Required Documentation and Procedures. (Pending DoD CIO additional guidance regarding DODIN Waivers).

C.3. Point of Contact. For further information, please contact: osd.pentagon.dod-cio.mbx.dcio-cs-ae@mail.mil

This page intentionally left blank

APPENDIX D: CLOUD POINTS OF CONTACT

Table 6: DoD Component Cloud Migration Office Points of Contact

COMPONENT	POC	CONTACT INFORMATION
Department of the Army	Army Application Migration Business Office (AAMBO) [27]	Unclassified Email: usarmy.belvoir.peo-eis.mbx.army-app-migration-office@mail.mil Website for the Army Application Migration Pre-assessment Tool: https://aampt.army.mil/aampt/main.do#/
Department of the Navy	Commercial Hosting Lead: Data Center Application Optimization (DCAO)/PEO EIS	Unclassified Email: Spawar-dcao-esm.FCM@navy.mil
U.S. Marine Corps	USMC HQMC C4	E-mail address HQMC_C4_MCCLOUD@usmc.mil Phone 703-693-3488
Department of the Air Force	Managed Service Office, MSO	Website: https://intelshare.intelink.gov/sites/afcce/SitePages/Home.aspx Phone: 334-416-3674
Defense Logistics Agency	DISA Liaison and Hosting Office Supporting DLA	Phone: 703-767-6900 703-767-9609 703-767-2198
Office of the Secretary of Defense / Joint Staff National Capital Region	Joint Service Provider (JSP) Pentagon Service Desk	Your organization's JSP Customer Account Manager or the JSP Service Desk at Unclassified Email: EITSDCustServices@osd.mil, Phone: 703-571-4577

---

[27] For an AAMBO introduction and overview see:
https://disa.deps.mil/ext/CloudServicesSupport/CCPG/AAMBO%20Introduction%20(AUGUST2015).pdf
In addition to the steps outlined in this *DoD Cloud Connection Process Guide*, Army Mission Owners are expected to follow the 6 Step Application Migration Process published in the Secretary of the Army Directive 2016-XX, *Migration of Army Systems and Applications to Approved Hosting Environments and Consolidation of Data Centers located at* https://army.deps.mil/army/cmds/hqda_ciog6_Project/ADCCP/CloudDocRepository/Documents/1604194822%20Signed%20SECARMY%20Army%20Directive%202016-38.pdf

Table 7: DISA Cloud Computing Team Points of Contact

DISA CLOUD COMPUTING TEAM	CONTACT INFORMATION
Cloud Services Support Office (CSSO)	Unclassified Email: disa.meade.re.mbx.disa-commercial-cloud@mail.mil Website: https://disa.deps.mil/ext/CloudServicesSupport/Pages/default.aspx Phone: 301-225-4530
Cybersecurity Service Provider (CSSP) Office (formerly Computer Network Defense Service Provider)	Unclassified email: disa.letterkenny.re.list.cdsp-requests@mail.mil Website: https://disa.deps.mil/ext/cop/fso/cndsp_PM/Lists/CNDSP%20POCs/AllItems.aspx
Customer Engagement Office Contact Information	Mission Partner Engagement Office Chief 301-225-5303, DSN: 375-5303 Deputy Chief 717-605-1492, DSN: 430-1492 Engagement Support Chief 301-225-7228, DSN: 375-7228 DISA Global Service Desk (24x7) 1-844-347-2457 Engagement Support Email Address: Disa.meade.bd.mbx.bdm4.mpeo.support@mail.mil Mission Partner Portal https://disa.deps.mil/ext/cop/cpp/home.aspx
DISA Cloud Assessment Team (CAT)	Phone: 301-225-3136 Unclassified email: disa.meade.re.mbx.cloud-team@mail.mil
DISA Command Center (DCC)	Website: https://disa.deps.mil/ORG/OP3/default.aspx
DISA CONUS Provisioning Center	Unclassified Email: PROVTMS@Scott.DISA.mil

DISA CLOUD COMPUTING TEAM (continued)	CONTACT INFORMATION
DISN Connection Approval Office	Unclassified Email: disa.meade.ns.mbx.ucao@mail.mil Phone: 301-225-2900/2901 or DSN 312-375-2900/2901
DSAWG Secretariat	Unclassified Email: disa.meade.re.mbx.dsawg@mail.mil Website: https://intelshare.intelink.gov/sites/dsawg/default.aspx Phone: 301-225-2905
Network Information Center (NIC)	For all unclassified connections contact the NIC through the DISA Customer Contact Center (DCCC) Unclassified Email: disa.dccc@mail.mil Website: https://www.nic.mil Phone: (844) 347-2457, Option 2; (614) 692-0032, Option 2; DSN: (312) 850-0032, Option 2
PPSM Configuration Control Board (CCB)/Technical Advisory Group	Phone: 301-225-2904
Web Content Filtering Office	Unclassified Email: disa.meade.ma.list.wcftieriii@mail.mil
DISA Cyber Authorization and Compliance Division (RE2)	Unclassified Email: disa.meade.re.list.cloud-ao-team@mail.mil
DoD IT Project Transitioning to the Cloud	https://disa.deps.mil/ext/CloudServicesSupport/Lists/Transitioning%20DoD%20Cloud%20IT%20Projects%20CITP/AllItems.aspx

This page intentionally left blank

APPENDIX E: ACRONYMS

ACRONYM	`DEFINITION
AT&L	Acquisition, Technology, and Logistics
ATC	NIPRNet Approval to Connect
ATO	Authorization to Operate
BCA	Business Case Analysis
BCAP	Boundary Cloud Access Point
CAO	Connection Approval Office
CAP	Cloud Access Point
CATC	Cloud Authorization to Connect
CCPG	Cloud Connection Process Guide
CCSD	Command Communications Service Designator
CIO	Chief Information Officer
C-ITP	Cloud Information Technology Project
CPTC	Cloud Permission to Connect
CSO	Cloud Service Offering
CSP	Cloud Service Provider
CSSP	Cyber Security Service Provider
CTM	Consent to Monitor
DCC	DISA Command Center
DDSF	DISA Direct Store Front
DISA	Defense Information Systems Agency
DISN	Defense Information Systems Network
DMZ	De-Militarized Zone
DODIN	Department of Defense Information Network
DSAWG	Defense Security/Cybersecurity Authorization Working Group
FedRAMP	Federal Risk and Authorization Management Program
GIAP	GIG Interconnection Approval Process

ACRONYM	`DEFINITION
GIG	Global Information Grid
IAP	Internet Access Point
ICAP	Internal Cloud Access Point
IIL	Information Impact Level
ISRMC	Information Security Risk Management Committee
IT	Information Technology
JRSS	Joint Regional Security Stack
JSP	Joint Services Provider (Pentagon)
MCD	Mission Cyber Defense
NFG	NIPRNet Federated Gateway
PA	Provisional Authorization
PM	Program Manager
POA&M	Plan of Actions and Milestones
POC	Points of Contact
PPSM	Ports, Protocols, and Services Management
RMF	Risk Management Framework
SAP	Security Assessment Plan
SAR	Security Assessment Report
SGS	SIPRNet GIAP System
SLA	Service Level of Agreement
SNAP	System Network Approval Process (Registers DISN connections)
SNaP-IT	Select & Native Programming Data Input System for Information Technology (SNaP-IT) (Registers DoD Department IT investments)
SSP	System Security Plan

APPENDIX F: DEFINITIONS

TERM	DEFINITION
Acknowledgement of Registration	An Acknowledgement of Registration is issued by DISA CSSO for CSP-CSO's that has a DoD PA, is registered in DISA SNAP, and connects to the NIPRNet: (1) from the Internet via an IAP, or (2) via a DoD Component CAP, or, (3) via an ICAP (On-Premise).
Approval to Connect (ATC)	An ATC is a formal statement by the DISA Connection Approval Office (CAO) granting approval of a circuit used by an enclave to connect to the NIPRNet. The CAO will grant a NIPRNet ATC for no more than three years. (Not to be confused with a Cloud Approval to Connect (CATC).)
Artifacts	System policies, documentation, plans, test procedures, test results, and other evidence that express or enforce the information assurance (IA)/cybersecurity posture of the DOD IS, make up the certification and accreditation (C&A)/assessment and authorization (A&A) information, and provide evidence of compliance with the assigned cybersecurity controls.
Authorization Decision	A formal statement by an Authorizing Official (AO) regarding acceptance of the risk associated with operating a DoD information system (IS) and expressed as an authorization to operate (ATO), interim authorization to test (IATT), or denial of ATO (DATO). The AO may issue the authorization decision in hard copy with a traditional signature or sign it electronically with a DoD Public Key Infrastructure (PKI)-certified digital signature.
Authorization Termination Date (ATD)	The date assigned by the AO that indicates when an ATO or IATT expires.

TERM	DEFINITION
Authorizing Official (AO)	Senior (federal) official or executive with the authority to formally assume responsibility for operating an information system at an acceptable level of risk to organizational operations (including mission, functions, image, or reputation), organizational assets, individuals, other organizations, and the Nation. (CNSSI No. 4009 (ref dd)). This term is synonymous with Designated Approving Authority (DAA) and Delegated Accrediting Authority (DAA).
Authorization to Operate (ATO)	The official management decision given by a senior organizational official to authorize operation of an information system and to explicitly accept the risk to organizational operations (including mission, functions, image, or reputation), organizational assets, individuals, other organizations, and the Nation based on the implementation of an agreed-upon set of security controls. (CNSSI No. 4009 (ref dd))
Certification	A comprehensive evaluation and validation of a DOD IS to establish the degree to which it complies with assigned cybersecurity controls based on standardized procedures. Note: DoDI 8510.01 Risk Management Framework transitions DoD from "certification and accreditation" to "assess and authorize."
Cloud Access Point	A system of network boundary protection and monitoring devices, otherwise known as a cybersecurity stack, through which CSP infrastructure will connect to a DoD Information Network (DODIN) service, the NIPRNet, or the Secret Internet Protocol Router Network (SIPRNet).
Cloud Approval to Connect (CATC)	A CATC is a formal statement by the DISA CAO granting approval for a Cloud Service Provider (CSP) to be connected to the DISN via a DISA BCAP. The CAO will not issue a CATC for longer than the period of validity of the associated DoD PA. The CAO will grant CATC for no more than three years duration. See Section 2 of this guide.
Cloud Broker	A proxy on behalf of cloud customers

TERM	DEFINITION
Cloud Computing	Cloud computing is a model for enabling ubiquitous, convenient, on-demand network access to a shared pool of configurable computing resources (e.g., networks, servers, storage, applications, and services) that can be rapidly provisioned and released with minimal management effort or service provider interaction. (NIST SP 800-145 (ref ee))
Cloud Denial To Connect (CDTC)	A CDTC is a formal statement by the Connection Approval Office withholding or rescinding approval for a CSP-CSO to connect (or remain connected) to the DISN.
Cloud Permission To Connect (CPTC)	A formal statement by the DISA Connection Approval Office granting approval for a Mission Owner to connect a C-ITP to a CSP-CSO via a DISA BCAP. DISA CSSO will grant a CPTC for no more than three years duration.
Cloud Service Provider-Cloud Service Offering (CSP-CSO)	A CSP-CSO is the IaaS/PaaS/SaaS solution available from a CSP. A CSP may provide several different CSP-CSOs.
Cloud Service Provider (CSP)	A CSP is a DoD or non-DoD entity that offers one or more cloud computing services in one or more deployment models. A CSP might leverage or outsource services of other organizations and other CSPs (e.g., placing certain servers or equipment in third party facilities such as data centers, carrier hotels / collocation facilities, and Internet Network Access Points (NAPs)). CSPs offering SaaS may leverage one or more third party CSP's (i.e., for IaaS or PaaS) to build out a capability or offering. • Commercial vendor or Federal organization offering or providing cloud computing services (Includes DoD CSPs) • Provides CSP-CSOs for mission use • Provides Cyber Defense services (all tiers) for its infrastructure and service offerings (DoD Cloud SRG (ref d))
Command Communications Service Designator (CCSD)	A CCSD is a unique identifier for each single service including use circuits, package system circuits, and inter-switch trunk circuits.

TERM	DEFINITION
Community Cloud	A Community Cloud is an infrastructure provided by a CSP for exclusive use by a specific community of Mission Owners from organizations that have shared concerns (e.g., mission, security requirements, policy, and compliance considerations). It may be owned, managed, and operated by one or more of the organizations in the community, a third party, or some combination of them, and it may exist On-Premise or Off-Premise. (NIST SP 800-145 (ref ee))
Continuous Monitoring	Maintaining ongoing awareness to support organizational risk decisions. CNSSI No. 4009 (ref dd)
Conditional Provisional Authorization	A Conditional DoD PA includes conditions for using a CSP-CSO, for example: • A requirement to use a CSP-CSO in conjunction with another CSP-CSO(s). • A requirement to use the CSP-CSO only in a specific environment or configuration.
Connection Approval Office (CAO)	Single point of contact within DISA for DISN connection approval requests.
Consent to Monitor (CTM)	This is the agreement signed by the AO granting DISA permission to periodically monitor the connection and assess the level of compliance with cybersecurity policy and guidelines.
Cybersecurity	Prevention of damage to, protection of, and restoration of computers, electronic communications systems, electronic communications services, wire communication, and electronic communication, including information contained therein, to ensure its availability, integrity, authentication, confidentiality, and nonrepudiation.

TERM	DEFINITION
Cyber Security Service Provider (CSSP)	An organization that provides one or more cybersecurity services to implement and protect the DODIN. The DoD Component-owned or -operated portion of the DODIN will be aligned with a Network Operations Security Center (NOSC) and an integrated capability to conduct cybersecurity activities. This cybersecurity capability may be obtained from within a DoD Component or from an authorized external DoD Component service provider. All service providers must be authorized in accordance with DoD O-8530.1-M, "Department of Defense Computer Network Defense (CND) Service Provider Certification and Accreditation Program," December 17, 2003 per DoDI 8530.01 of 07 March 2016) (ref hh).
Defense Security/Cybersecurity Authorization Working Group (DSAWG)	Provides, interprets, and approves the DISN security policy, guides architecture development, and recommends accreditation decisions to the DoD ISRMC. Also reviews and approves Cross Domain information transfers (when delegated by the ISRMC), or forwards such recommendation(s) to the ISRMC.
Defense Information Systems Agency (DISA) Store Front	This is the ordering tool for DISN telecommunications services. (Formerly DISA Direct Order Entry (DDOE))
Defense Information Systems Network Connection Process Guide	The DISN CPG is a step-by-step guide to the detailed procedures that Partners must follow in order to obtain and retain connections to the DISN. (ref f)
Defense Information Systems Network (DISN)	DOD integrated network, centrally managed and configured to provide long-haul information transfer for all Department of Defense activities. It is an information transfer utility designed to provide dedicated point-to-point, switched voice and data, imagery and video teleconferencing services.

TERM	DEFINITION
Demilitarized Zone (DMZ)	1. Perimeter network segment that is logically between internal and external networks. Its purpose is to enforce the internal network's Information Assurance (IA) policy for external information exchange and to provide external, untrusted sources with restricted access to releasable information while shielding the internal networks from outside attacks. 2. A host or network segment inserted as a "neutral zone" between an organization's private network and the Internet. 3. An interface on a routing firewall that is similar to the interfaces found on the firewall's protected side. Traffic moving between the DMZ and other interfaces on the protected side of the firewall still goes through the firewall and can have firewall protection policies applied. (CNSSI No. 4009 (ref dd))
Denial of Approval to Connect (DATC)	A formal statement by the Connection Approval Office withholding (in the case of a new connection request) or rescinding (in the case of a reaccreditation connection) approval for an IS to connect (or remain connected) to the DISN.
Denial of Authorization to Operate (DATO)	A DATO is an AO decision that a DOD IS cannot operate because of an inadequate cybersecurity design, failure to adequately implement assigned cybersecurity controls, or other lack of adequate security. If the system is already operational, the operation of the system is halted.
Department of Defense Information Network (DODIN)	The globally interconnected, end-to-end set of information capabilities, and associated processes for collecting, processing, storing, disseminating, and managing information on-demand to warfighters, policy makers, and support personnel, including owned and leased communications and computing systems and services, software (including applications), data, and security." (DoDI 8110.01)
Department of Defense Information Security Risk Management Committee (ISRMC)	The DoD ISRMC, comprised of the four mission area Principal Authorizing Officials (PAOs) and other major DoD and Intelligence Community (IC) stakeholders, provides the Tier 1 [Organizational] risk management governance for DoD. (DoDI 8500.01)

TERM	DEFINITION
Designated Accrediting Authority (DAA)	"Authorizing Official" supersedes this term.
DOD Information System (IS)	Set of information resources organized for the collection, storage, processing, maintenance, use, sharing, dissemination, disposition, display, or transmission of information. It includes automated information system (AIS) applications, enclaves, outsourced IT-based processes, and platform IT interconnections.
DODIN Readiness and Security Inspections (DRSI)	Produces and deploys information assurance (IA) products, services, and capabilities to combatant commands, services, and agencies to protect and defend the DODIN.
Enclave	A set of system resources that operate in the same security domain and that share the protection of a single, common, continuous security perimeter. (CNSSI No. 4009 (ref dd))
Hybrid Cloud	The cloud infrastructure is a composition of two or more distinct cloud infrastructures (private, community, or public) that remain unique entities, but are bound together by standardized or proprietary technology that enables data and application portability (e.g., cloud bursting for load balancing between clouds). (NIST SP 800-145 (ref ee))
Information Impact Level (IIL)	Cloud security information impact levels (e.g., High, Moderate, or Low) are defined by the combination of: 1) the sensitivity or confidentiality level of information (e.g., public, private, classified, etc.) to be stored and processed in the CSP environment; and 2) the potential impact of an event that results in the loss of confidentiality, integrity, or availability of that information. (DoD Cloud SRG (ref d))

TERM	DEFINITION
Information Systems (IS)	A discrete set of information resources organized for the collection, processing, maintenance, use, sharing, dissemination, or disposition of information. (44 U.S.C. Sec 3502) Note: Information systems also include specialized systems such as industrial/process controls systems, telephone switching and private branch exchange (PBX) systems, and environmental control systems. (CNSSI No. 4009 (ref dd)
Infrastructure as a Service (IaaS)	The capability provided to the Mission Owner is to provision processing, storage, networks, and other fundamental computing resources where the Mission Owner is able to deploy and run arbitrary software, which can include operating systems and applications. The Mission Owner does not manage or control the underlying cloud infrastructure but has control over operating systems, storage, and deployed applications; and possibly limited control of select networking components (e.g., host firewalls). (NIST SP 800-145 (ref ee))
Interim Approval to Connect (IATC)	Temporary approval granted by the Connection Approval Office for the connection of an IS to the DISN under the conditions or constraints enumerated in the connection approval.
Interim Authorization to Test (IATT)	Temporary authorization to test an information system in a specified operational information environment within the timeframe and under the conditions or constraints enumerated in the written authorization. (CNSSI No. 4009 (ref dd))

TERM	DEFINITION
Internal Cloud Access Point (ICAP)	An ICAP capability for the NIPRNet provides interconnection between a commercial CSP infrastructure at any impact Level 2-5 (dedicated to DoD) located inside the Base/Camp/Post/Station "fence-line" (i.e., On-Premise). The may leverage existing capabilities such as the IA Stack protecting a DoD Data center today, JIE Core Data Center (CDC) tomorrow, or may be part of a Joint Regional Security Stack (JRSS). In addition, an ICAP may have special capabilities to support specific missions, CSP types (commercial or DoD), or specific cloud services. ICAP implementation and the connection of an On-Premise CSP-CSO infrastructure to the NIPRNet will follow the normal NIPRNet connection approval guidance and requirements in the DISN CPG (ref f).
Internet Access Point (IAP).	An IAP establishes a protected boundary between the NIPRNet and the public Internet. An IAP has capabilities to detect and prevent a cyber-attack on the NIPRNet from the Internet.
Internet Protocol (IP)	Standard protocol for transmission of data from source to destinations in packet-switched communications networks and interconnected systems of such networks. (CNSSI No. 4009 (ref dd))
Joint Services Provider (JSP) - Pentagon	JSP provides Cloud Cyberspace Defense services for designated DoD Components in the National Capital Region that use the JSP private AWS GovCloud service. For additional information, contact your Organization's JSP Customer Account Manager (CAM) or the JSP Service Desk.
Limited Provisional Authorization	Limits the period of validity of the PA to less than three years and/or limits the C-ITPs permitted to use the CSP-CSO. a. If a DoD Limited PA will be permanently limited to one or more DoD Component(s) then the authorized Component(s) will be listed on the PA Memo. b. If a DoD Limited PA is not permanently limited, the PA memo will state that a component will seek the additional authorization to onboard from the DISA AO via the established AO Authorization process.

TERM	DEFINITION
Meet-Me-Points	Meet-Me-Points provide a full range of premium collocation, interconnection and support services to a wide range of networks, enterprise and content companies. DISA locates the Meet-Me-Points at contractor facilities where many CSPs are located.
Mission Owner	Entities such as IT system/application owner/operators or program managers within the DoD Components/Agencies responsible for instantiating and operating one or more information systems and applications who may leverage a CSP's CSO in fulfilment of IT missions. (DoD Cloud SRG (ref d))
Mission Partners	Those with whom Department of Defense cooperates to achieve national goals, such as other departments and agencies of the U.S. Government; state and local governments, allies, coalition members, host nations and other nations; multinational organizations; non-governmental organizations; and the private sector.
Approval to Connect (ATC)	A NIPRNet ATC is a formal statement by the DISA Connection Approval Office (CAO) granting approval of a circuit used by an n enclave to connect to the NIPRNet. The CAO will grant a NIPRNet ATC for no more than three years.
Off-Boarding	Off-boarding is the set of activities that take place when a Mission Owner discontinues use of a CSP-CSO. An off-boarding process is required when a Mission Owner migrates to a new cloud service, a mission reaches end of life, a contract ends, or a CSP-CSO ceases operations. (DoD Cloud SRG (ref d))
On-Boarding	On-boarding is the set of activities that take place when a Mission Owner migrates a C-ITP to an authorized CSP-CSO.
Plan of Action & Milestones (POA&M)	A document that identifies tasks needing to be accomplished. It details resources required to accomplish the elements of the plan, any milestones in meeting the tasks, and scheduled completion dates for the milestones. (CNSSI No. 4009 (ref dd))

TERM	DEFINITION
Platform as a Service (PaaS)	The capability provided to the Mission Owner is to deploy onto the cloud infrastructure Mission Owner - created or acquired applications created using programming languages, libraries, services, and tools supported by the provider. The Mission Owner does not manage or control the underlying cloud infrastructure including network, servers, operating systems, or storage, but has control over the deployed applications and possibly configuration settings for the application-hosting environment. (NIST SP 800-145 (ref ee))
Private Cloud	The cloud infrastructure is provisioned for exclusive use by a single organization comprising multiple Mission Owner s (e.g., business units). It may be owned, managed, and operated by the organization, a third party, or some combination of them, and it may exist On-Premise or Off-Premise. (NIST SP 800-145 (ref ee))
Program or System Manager (PM or SM)	A PM or SM is the individual with responsibility for and authority to accomplish program or system objectives for development, production, and sustainment to meet the user's operational needs.
Provisional Authorization (DoD)	A DoD Provisional Authorization (PA) is an acceptance of risk based on an evaluation of the CSPs offering and the potential for risk introduced to DoD networks. It provides a foundation that Authorizing Officials (AOs) responsible for mission applications can leverage in determining the overall risk to the missions/applications that are executed as part of a CSP-CSO. (DoD Cloud SRG (ref d)) – See "Limited Provisional Authorization" and "Conditional Provisional Authorization."
Public Cloud	The cloud infrastructure is provisioned for open use by the public. It may be owned, managed, and operated by a business, academic, or government organization, or some combination of them. It exists on the premises of the cloud provider. (NIST SP 800-145 (ref ee))
Request For Service (RFS)	The document submitted to the TCO to request telecommunications service.

TERM	DEFINITION
Security Assessment Plan (SAP)	The SAP provides the objectives for the security control assessment and a detailed roadmap of how to conduct such an assessment. (DoDI-8510.01)
Security Assessment Report (SAR)	The SAR provides a disciplined and structured approach for documenting the findings of the assessor and the recommendations for correcting any identified vulnerabilities in the security controls. [DoDI 8510.01]
Select & Native Programming Data Input System for Information Technology (SNaP-IT)	SNaP-IT is the authoritative Department of Defense (DoD) database used for publishing the DoD Information Technology (IT) Budget Estimates to Congress, the Circular A-11 Section 53 and Section 300 exhibits to the Office of Management and Budget (OMB), and for monthly IT performance reporting to the OMB IT Dashboard. The DoD CIO operates the SNaP-IT system. Additional SNaP-IT guidance can be located within the DoD Financial Management Regulation (7000.14-R, Volume 2B, Chapter 18) or within annual budget guidance issued by OUSD(C), D, CAPE, and DoD CIO.
Significant Change	NIST SP 800-37 defines a *significant change* as a change that is likely to affect the security state of an information system. Significant changes to an information system may include for example: (i) installation of a new or upgraded operating system, middleware component, or application; (ii) modifications to system ports, protocols, or services; (iii) installation of a new or upgraded hardware platform; (iv) modifications to cryptographic modules or services; or (v) modifications to security controls. Examples of significant changes to the environment of operation may include for example: (i) moving to a new facility; (ii) adding new core missions or business functions; (iii) acquiring specific and credible threat information that the organization is being targeted by a threat source; or (iv) establishing new/modified laws, directives, policies, or regulations. The examples of changes listed above are only *significant* when a change is likely to affect the security state of the information system.

TERM	DEFINITION
Software as a Service (SaaS)	The capability provided to the Mission Owner is to use the provider's applications running on a cloud infrastructure. The applications are accessible from various client devices through either a thin client interface, such as a web browser (e.g., web-based email), or a program interface. The Mission Owner does not manage or control the underlying cloud infrastructure including network, servers, operating systems, storage, or even individual application capabilities, with the possible exception of limited user-specific application configuration settings. (NIST SP 800-145 (ref ee))
Sponsor (DoD)	DoD component responsible for ensuring the connection or CSP-CSO has a valid DoD mission essential requirement to be connected to the DISN. The DoD Sponsor and DoD Mission Owner can be one in the same. The responsibilities of DoD Sponsor for a CSP-CSO will be stipulated in future versions of this guide.)
Systems Security Plan (SSP)	Formal document that provides an overview of the security requirements for an information system and describes the security controls in place or planned for meeting those requirements. [NIST-SP 800-18]
Virtual Private Network (VPN)	Protected information system link utilizing tunneling, security controls, and endpoint address translation giving the impression of a dedicated line. (CNSSI No. 4009 (ref dd)) DoD enterprise VPN services are described at: http://www.disa.mil/Network-Services/VPN
Virtual Routing and Forwarding (VRF)	A technology that allows multiple routing tables to exist within the same router/switch. Provides the ability to support communities of interest, separate applications, and coalitions on a single physical network.

This page intentionally left blank

APPENDIX G: RESPONSIBILITIES

G.1 DISA Enterprise BCAP Connection Responsibilities

This section only addresses roles and responsibilities after the CSP receives a Cloud Approval to Connect (CATC) to the DISA Enterprise BCAP from the DISA Connection Approval Office (CAO). The key stakeholders are DISA Enterprise BCAP Program Manager/Service Manager, DISA IP Tier 3 Engineers, DISA Global NetOps Support Center (GNSC), transport and DoD contracted Meet-Me-Point provider, and CSPs.

G.3.1 DISA Enterprise BCAP Program Manager/Service Manager

The Program Manager or Service Manager is responsible for planning, budgeting, and providing overall network policy and guidance. Specific duties include:

a. Analyze/concur/approve new CSP connection

b. Approve operating system and hardware life-cycle support and upgrades

c. Analyze/concur/approve funding for new equipment, new DISA Enterprise BCAP site(s) and backbone bandwidth requirements

d. Provide annual funding for the operations, hardware life-cycle support and upgrade of the DISA Enterprise BCAP including circuits

G.1.2 DISA IP Tier 3 Engineers

The DISA IP Tier 3 Engineers are responsible for overall network architectural design and network evolution of the DISA Enterprise BCAP. The DISN IP Tier 3 Engineers also assist in troubleshooting analysis of DISA Enterprise BCAP outages. Specific duties in the CSP-CSO Connection Process include:

a. Responsible for network architecture and long range network planning

b. Perform requirement analysis of the CSP connection to the DISA Enterprise CAP

c. Recommend router configuration on the Meet-Me-Point for each CSP activation

d. Evaluate/Analyze/Recommend new equipment, new DISA Enterprise BCAP site(s) and backbone bandwidth requirements

e. Recommend operating system and hardware life-cycle support and upgrades

f. Provide assistance to DISA GNSC and the DoD contracted transport provider during troubleshooting of complex problems/outages

G.1.3 DISA GNSC

The DISA GNSC is responsible for the management and operations of the DISA Enterprise Infrastructure to ensure delivery of services and capabilities in support of the Combatant Commands, Service Branches, and DoD Agencies. Specific duties in the CSP-CSO Connection Process include:

a. Coordinate the requirement analysis of the CSP connection to the DISA Enterprise CAP

b. Participate in the Initial Testing and Acceptance (IT&A) of new CSP connections/circuits

c. Manage and maintain NFG configurations, access and permission levels for all users

d. Coordinate new equipment, DISA Enterprise BCAP site(s), and backbone bandwidth requirements

e. Coordinate router configuration on the Meet-Me-Point for each CSP activation

f. Provide assistance to the DoD contracted transport provider during troubleshooting of complex problems/outages

g. Coordinate operational assessment/testing with stakeholders

h. Perform day-to-day capacity planning (modeling). If a need for DISA Enterprise BCAP bandwidth or hardware is determined, it is engineered and forwarded to the Program Manager/Service Manager for concurrence/funding approval

i. Perform Initial Testing and Acceptance (IT&A) of new network elements and circuits

j. Escalate issues to the DISA IP Tier 3 Engineers to troubleshoot configuration issues and resolve problems

k. Coordinate network architecture and long range network planning

l. Coordinate operating system and hardware life-cycle support and upgrades

G.1.4 Meet-Me-Point Contractor

DISA BCAP Meet-Me-Points offer a full range of premium collocation, interconnection and support services to a wide range of networks, enterprise and content companies. DISA locates Meet-Me-Points at contractor facility where many CSPs are located. Specific duties in the CSP-CSO Connection Process include:

a. Coordinate the requirement analysis of the CSP connection to the DISA Enterprise CAP

b. Provide quotes to the CSP

c. Provide the cross connect between the CSP and the Meet Me Router

d. Coordinate engineering support with DISA, the contracted transport provider and CSP

e. Participate in IT&A with DISA, the DoD contracted transport provider and CSP

f. Provide power and space for the Meet-Me-Point under contract to the DoD contracted transport provider

G.1.5 CSPs

A CSP is a company that offers some component of cloud computing – typically Infrastructure as a Service (IaaS), Software as a Service (SaaS) or Platform as a Service (PaaS) – to businesses, agencies and services. Specific duties in the CSP-CSO Connection Process include:

a. Coordinate the requirement analysis of the CSP connection to the DISA Enterprise CAP

b. Coordinate the Meet-Me Router provisioning actions

c. Coordinate engineering support with DISA, the DoD contracted transport and Meet-Me-Point providers

d. Participate in IT&A with DISA, the contracted transport and Meet-Me-Point providers

Coordinate operational assessment/testing with stakeholders

- APPENDIX H: CLASSIFIED (INFORMATION IMPACT LEVEL 6) C-ITP REGISTRATION AND CONNECTION PROCESS

H.1 DoD authorizes a Level 6 CSP-CSO to accommodate information that has been determined to be classified national security information. The classification determination is pursuant to (i) Executive Order 13526, *Classified National Security Information* (December 29, 2009), or (ii) pursuant to the Atomic Energy Act of 1954, as amended, (P.L. 83-703)16 to be Restricted Data (RD).

H.2 At this time, only information classified as SECRET, in accordance with the applicable Executive Orders, is applicable to information impact level 6. DISA's MilCloud offers a SECRET IaaS/PaaS CSP-CSO connected to SIPRNet. [28]

H.3 The DISA MilCloud web site has instructions for registering, connecting, and on-boarding to a MilCloud CSP-CSO on SIPRNet. .

H.4 CSP-CSOs and C-ITPs running at classification levels above SECRET are outside the scope of this guide.

Mission Owners must register their Information Impact Level 6 (secret) DoD Cloud IT Projects in the SIPRNet GIAP System (SGS) when the SGS cloud module becomes available.

---

[28]Information about MilCloud is available at: http://www.disa.mil/Computing/Cloud-Services/MilCloud

This page intentionally left blank

APPENDIX I: SAMPLE OF AN IT TOPOLOGY DIAGRAM

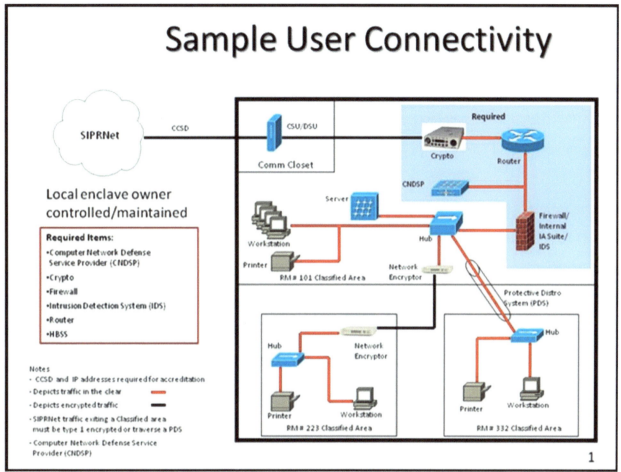

Figure 15: Sample Connectivity Topology Diagram

An IT Topology identifies equipment (e.g., XXX DSU/CSU; CISCO WC-1DSU-T1-V2-RF; Cisco 3600 Router; Cisco IDS 4210 Sensor, Cisco 4900 Catalyst Switch) and includes all IP addresses, etc. Figure 15 is an illustration from the DISN Connection Process Guide. Although Figure 15 illustrates a sample IT topology for a SIPRNet connection, it provides an example that can be used for illustrating an enclave connected to the NIPRNet.

This page intentionally left blank

APPENDIX J: INFORMATION REQUIREMENTS FOR CLOUD REGISTRATIONS AND CONNECTION REQUESTS

Documents and Information	CSO Registration	CSO CATC DISA BCAP Only	C-ITP Registration	C-ITP CPTC (DISA BCAP Only)	Verification Procedure
Business Case Analysis (BCA) see (ref c) **and** (ref w)			✓	✓	Self Validation by Cloud IT Project POC
Authorization to Operate (ATO) or Variant see (ref b)	If On-Premise in Gov't Space	If On-Premise in Gov't Space	✓	✓	Document Review and Analysis by Connection Approval Office
DoD PA	✓	✓	✓	✓	Validated by Connection Approval Office
FedRAMP ID	✓	✓	✓	✓	
Information Impact Level see (ref d)	✓	✓	✓	✓	Self Validation by the submitting POC
Cloud Service Model see (ref j)	✓	✓	✓	✓	
Cloud Deployment Model see (ref j)	✓	✓	✓	✓	
PPSM Registration Number(s) see (ref ff)	✓	✓	✓	✓	Database Check by CAP Engineering Team / Entries adopted into CAP own Registration
Whitelist Registration Number(s)[29]	✓	✓	✓	✓	Database Check by CAP Engineering Team / Entries adopted into CAP own Registration

---

[29] CSPs and Mission Owners must register in the NIPRNet DMZ Whitelist (ref m) any CSP-CSO connection that transits between the NIPRNet and the Internet.

Documents and Information	CSO Registration	CSO CATC DISA BCAP Only		C-ITP Registration	C-ITP CPTC (DISA BCAP Only)	Verification Procedure
Virtual Routing and Forwarding (VRF)/VPN ID see (ref f)	optional	optional		optional	optional	Database Check by CAP Engineering Team
CCSD Number (s) see (ref f) and (ref gg)	optional	optional		optional	optional	Database Check by CAP Engineering Team
DISA CSSO Verification				✓	✓	Notification Forwarded to Component , Acknowledgement Returned from Component
DoD CSO Initial Contact Form see (ref n)	✓	✓				Document Review and Analysis by CAP Engineering Team
DoD C-ITP Initial Contact Form see (ref x)				✓	✓	
Topology Diagram(s) see Appendix I	✓	✓		✓	✓	Document Review and Analysis by CAP Engineering Team
DoD Cloud IT Project Name				✓	✓	Self Validation by Cloud IT Project POC CSSO confirms same name as in SNaP-IT and DITPR
DoD C-IPT POC(s)				✓	✓	Self Validation by Cloud IT Project POC
DoD Sponsor POC(s) Info	✓	✓		(If non-DoD C-ITP)	(If non-DoD C-ITP)	Self Validation by Cloud IT Project POC

Documents and Information	CSO Registration	CSO CATC DISA BCAP Only	C-ITP Registration	C-ITP CPTC (DISA BCAP Only)	Verification Procedure
DoD Component Cloud migration office POCs Info see **Appendix D, Table 6**			(if required)	(if required)	
Consent-to-Monitor Agreement see Appendix K	✓	✓	✓	✓	Self Validation by Cloud IT Project POC
Cloud Service Provider POC(s) Info	✓	✓			Self Validation by Cloud Service Provider POC
DITPR Number(s) see (ref gg)			✓	✓	Self Validation by Cloud IT Project POC Database Check by CAP Engineering Team
SNaP-IT Number(s)			✓	✓	Self Validation by Cloud IT Project POC Database Check by CAP Engineering Team

Documents and Information	CSO Registration	CSO CATC DISA BCAP Only	C-ITP Registration	C-ITP CPTC (DISA BCAP Only)	Verification Procedure
CSP-CSO Name/Title	✓	✓	✓	✓	Selection Reviewed by Connection Approval Office regarding Restrictions of Use by PA – must match the name given in the DoD PA. Databases Checked by CAP Engineering Team
CSP Security Package Documentation Checklist see (ref o)	✓	✓		✓	
POA&M Document(s)		✓		✓	Document Review and Analysis by Connection Approval Office
CSSP SLA(s) see (ref hh)	✓	✓	✓	✓	Notification Forwarded to CNDSP, Acknowledgement Returned from CNDSP
Contract Number(s)			✓	✓	Self Validation by Cloud IT Project POC
IP Address(es)	✓	✓	✓	✓	Document Review and Analysis by CAP Engineering Team
CPTC Memo				✓	Content Verified by CAO
CATC Memo		✓			Content Verified by CAO

APPENDIX K: CONSENT TO MONITOR AGREEMENT (SAMPLE)

DEPARTMENT OF THE *<Service>*

<Address>

REPLY TO

ATTENTION OF:

The Consent To Monitor (CTM) is a mandatory document. The Mission Owner must submit a signed CTM to DISA (Defense Information Systems Agency) to complete the Cloud Connection Approval Package.

Cut and paste the text below, format as appropriate, and print on Organization Letterhead. Be sure to provide the Cloud Service Offering and Cloud IT Project names as appropriate...

When complete, Mission Owner will upload the CTM statement into the SNAP registration package.

Questions about the CTM may be directed to the Connection Approval Office at:

301-225-2900 or 301-225-2901 (DSN prefix is 312-)

Email: disa.meade.re.mbx.ucao@mail.mil

<Date>

SUBJECT: Consent to Monitor for *<CSP-CSO or C-ITP Name>*, CCSD *<Circuit, VPN or VRF Identifier (if any)>*

1. In accordance with the requirements of Chairman Joint Chief of Staff Instruction (CJCSI) 6211.02D, Defense Information Systems Network (DISN) Responsibilities, 24 January 2012, and Unclassified Connection Approval Office (UCAO) Requirements, I acknowledge that the Defense Information Systems Agency (DISA) will conduct periodic monitoring of the NIPRNet/IP Core/DATMS-U circuits. I acknowledge and consent to DISA conducting initial and periodic unannounced vulnerability assessments on our connected host system to determine the security features in place to protect against unauthorized access or attack.

Authorizing Official

This page intentionally left blank

This page intentionally left blank

Defense Information Systems Agency
Risk Adjudication and Connection (RE 4)
Post Office Box 549
Fort Meade, Maryland 20755-0549
http://disa.mil/connect